REAL LIFE NOTES

REAL LIFE NOTES

REFLECTIONS AND STRATEGIES FOR
LIFE AFTER GRADUATION

KENNETH JEDDING

DoubleRoseBooks
NEW YORK

Double Rose Books, Inc.
P.O. Box 180
New York, N.Y. 10276-0180
212 228-6650 800 253-4992 Fax 212 228-6632
www.doublerosebooks.com

Printed in the United States of America.

Library of Congress Card Number: 2001116044
ISBN 0-9678545-3-9

DRB logo: Kim Glassman

Real Life Notes is Book I of The Life Navigator Series™

To Bette

Contents

Introduction

You did it. You graduated. Congratulations!

Now you get to start the rest of your life. How does it feel?

Exciting?

Terrifying?

I used to think that there was a certain comfort to the school calendar. No matter what went right or wrong during the semester, it was followed by winter and summer breaks. And after those planned vacations, everything seemed to start over again, fresh. It was as simple as ordering food in a diner.

The waiter comes by. "What will you have?" he asks.

"...A burger, fries and a summer break please, because my roommate's a slob, my relationship's not going well, and my earliest class starts at 9:30."

(After a moment, delivering the food) "Here's your burger.....fries.....and your ticket home. We'll see you in September."

(Taking the food and the ticket) "I cannot begin to thank you."

So the bad news: After graduation, you're now conceivably in a world that will run straight through, one long life semester until you're wearing diapers and your grandchildren are embarrassed by the way you inadvertently dribble your food down your chin.

The good news: You may be entering the best part of your life. Whatever you develop for yourself that's good can remain that way until you decide to change it.

Everything is possible.

☆　　☆　　☆

WHY I WROTE THIS BOOK

I am forty-two. I first graduated twenty years ago. A few days after commencement, I walked into my college bookstore and said, "Could you please give me THE BOOK?"

"What book?" they asked.

"You know. THE BOOK," I said.

"What do you mean?"

"You know. The one that will give me a clue about the rest of my life: work, relationships, family, the whole thing."

"We've never heard of such a book."

"Well, what am I supposed to do, then?"

"We have no idea."

I left the bookstore.

My life was beginning and I didn't have a clue what to do with it. So I decided I'd develop my own little strategy. After all, you had to have a plan.

MY PLAN

—I'd worry as much as possible about my career and whatever else came to mind.
—I'd argue with my family.
—I'd get into short relationships that had no chance of working out.

Hmmm.
Well, at least I had a plan...

Other cultures handle things differently.

Many tribal cultures have initiation rituals. They care about how their young come to take their rightful place in society.

OK, but initiation rituals in those societies usually include such things as spending a month out in the rain forest. Or in isolation huts. Or getting beaten...or gored by wild animals.

That's the initiation fast track. But let's face it— aside from the Pacific Northwest, we don't have too many rain forests in this country, and even if we did, who's going to toss you out into one?

☆   ☆   ☆

Instead, here in America, the land of opportunity, your first opportunity after school is to get it right based on practically no information.

Our system was modeled on the idea of "Laissez-faire Capitalism." Laissez-faire means, in French, "to leave to do." It means leave it alone. So the plan is to leave the economic system alone, and to leave you alone to figure it out on your own.

Fine.

I figured it out the way most people do.

Here is an excerpt from the soundtrack of that experience:

AAW! OOOOHH!! Watch out!!!! Ouch!!!! Oh My God!!!! Now what?? Stitches. This again?? I've had it! Duck!!!

☆   ☆   ☆

Time passed. Many of the questions I had were answered.

Then one day I found myself in a mentoring program, trying to give something back. And talking to a guy named Matt, I realized I still had questions, but they'd changed over the years. New issues had taken the place of the ones I'd had to deal with after graduating from school. Yet, he was interested in those questions that I now took for granted. And it suddenly occurred to me to write it all down.

This book was inspired by that mentoring experience, in the belief that certain things need to be said.

Some of what's in this book will be useful for you.

Some may sound like common sense, but it may not be that common. For example, common wisdom says that it's best to pursue the career you like, nothing new there, but why then don't most people do it? This book presents some of those familiar ideas in a new light.

And finally, some of it may not apply to you at all.

Here's the thing: This book is full of ideas and strategies. Any one of them can save you months...or years. Just as if you're on a boat and you shift one degree in a better direction, two hours later you'll be not merely inches but miles closer to where you're going.

Chapter One

On Career

On Not Getting Stuck

Like many people, when I graduated from college I had a problem. I didn't know exactly what to do, but I knew I had to take action. I worried about going in the wrong direction and then getting stuck wherever I ended up. In the fantasy, I'd turn sixty and still be grinding away, thinking, "If I'd only known what to do after school, I wouldn't have wasted my life this way."

Now I see that I didn't need to worry about getting stuck and you don't either, for several reasons.

First, the belief that you might get stuck is based on a misperception of time and space; the idea that in order to move forward you need full knowledge, information, and self-awareness—that you need to know exactly where you're going, or else how can you possibly get there?

But consider this: If you were 100% sure of precisely where you were heading before you set out, the actual "working" aspect would be mechanical, even robotic. Nothing new would be added: no new learning, no unexpected information, surprise, or fun. And if this were really the ideal, how could your future career possibly fill you with excitement? Dread or boredom would be more like it!

> *The perfectly known future is a past.*
> — *Joseph Campbell*

The wheels turn in a different way.

You set out to do something, and in the process you refine your concept of what it is you really want to do. Life's an active feedback loop: The path you take sends back information that helps you adjust and revise...the path you'll take. Your career teaches you about your career: what it can be and also what you want it to be.

So what does this have to do with getting stuck? The idea is this: Even if you start in the wrong direction, or on the opposite course from the one you'll eventually follow, the information you receive on the way will be worth more to you than any possible downside.

All you need to do now is use the best idea you have about who you are and the direction you want to take, and then make a move. Balance action with reflection, but take action—even if you have limited knowledge of exactly where it will all lead. And of course, keep your eyes open.

Think of it this way: Imagine that at graduation, you're given a rowboat but no oars. Using your best idea at the time, you somehow float to the first job in your career—even as you are first defining what that career actually is. And at this job, in addition to the financial compensation, you gain another benefit: you somehow make yourself the first oar.

As a result, you're better able to chart the course to where you should logically "row" yourself next, whether laterally in the same company or field, or into another area altogether.

The key: Your experience is not the only thing that grows in time. Your perspective does as well.

Sometimes it is more important to discover what one cannot do, than what one can do.
— Lin Yutang

It is a mistake to look too far ahead. Only one link in the chain of destiny can be handled at a time. — Winston Churchill

Another reason you don't need to worry is this: Getting stuck is much harder than it used to be!

In the corporate culture of years past, people framed their lives in terms of getting stuck. That was their dream! It was considered bad form to have too many job changes on your resume, and people hoped to stay with the same companies, in the same careers, day in and day out until retirement.

Things have changed.

Now the bottom line is that even if you *wanted* to stay in one job, or even one career, the American economy doesn't carry workers the way it once did. If you aren't motivated by the work you're doing, you won't likely be working happily or productively. In that case, if you don't choose to leave out of sheer boredom or despair, the company might prefer someone else who was more dynamically motivated. Either way, through your own initiative or by your own default, you'd have to change.

This point may be hard to factor in when you're getting used to a new, entry-level job, in which you have plenty of time to kill—as people often do in entry-level—and you're waiting for the proverbial osmosis to set in. I'll have more on entry-level later.

For now, here's the thing: While this economy no longer carries people as it once did, it allows for greater mobility. So wherever you begin, trust that you'll learn what you need to learn, and then surely move on.

Even in science we cannot know. We can only do. — *Goethe*

The only source of knowledge is experience. — *Albert Einstein*

☆   ☆   ☆

One final point about getting stuck.

Your career doesn't define who you are. We like to say we're lawyers, we're stockbrokers, we're this, we're that. But if you ever went to a career counselor, she wouldn't see you that way, but would be more concerned with your skill sets.

In many computer paint programs, you can point and click on a spot on a color wheel, and the program scans the color and translates it into numerical values of its component colors; for example, red, green, and blue. So let's say I see a Sky Blue I like. It's not really a "blue," quantitatively speaking, but may actually be 38 red, 44 green and 89 blue.

In the same way, instead of thinking of a career as the label (doctor, lawyer, business, creative...), think of how it would scan for skill sets. Taking the legal profession as an example, the "red" "green" and "blue" categories might include Logical Thinking, Negotiating, Problem Solving, Articulating and Arguing Positions, Organizing, and Politics.

Therefore if Tom starts out as an associate in a law firm and then he stops, his real question would be, "Which of these skills have I developed, and where else can I apply them?"

Let's say Tom's self-evaluation of his experience is as follows: Logical Thinking 60, Negotiating 0, Problem Solving 15, Articulating and Arguing positions 0, and Politics 25.

That would be the true measure of what the job is for Tom.

He wouldn't be taking these readings from any objective scale—but since he knows that negotiating plays no part, he gives it a 0. Logical thinking is the greatest factor in his everyday life at work, so he gives it a 60. *The degree to which these scores correspond to his inner ideal is the degree to which he'll feel happy and motivated in his work.*

Let's say that his scores are out of sync with his ideals. In fact, his inner template includes categories that don't even come into play. He'd like to have a flexible schedule, for example, so that's a necessary category. But since his job is a 9 to 5, he'd grade himself a 0 in that new "Flexible Schedule" category—if he included it at all. Also, he'd like to be negotiating and he's not, so he gave himself a 0 in that one as well.

Again, if there's a big gap between his ideal scores and the ones he's pulling in here, the experience will be the opposite of that which will make him feel happy and motivated. And the degree to which those scores are out of alignment with his ideal is the degree to which he'll need to move on. More on the color scanning categories below.

For now, remember this: When he finally changes jobs, the skills he has developed are what he'll take with him more than any label.

The secret of success is to be ready when your opportunity comes. — *Benjamin Disraeli*

Wherever we are, it is but a stage on the way to somewhere else, and whatever we do, however well we do it, it is only a preparation to do something else that shall be different.
— *Robert Louis Stevenson*

Making Money

For many graduates, the main goal is to make money. There's great value to financial independence, from paying off a mountain of school debt to living the good life. Yet if this is your primary motivation, your first real step is identical to that of people whose priorities are different: Knowing who you are.

Without knowing who you are, if your goal is to earn money, you may ask the logical question, "Where's the money?" ...And then turn to some of the most obvious answers: in finance, in real estate and even in information technology. But these answers can be deceiving. They may apply generally but not always specifically, and you're a specific individual. In other words, these may not be the best areas for *you* to make money.

The truth is, people have made money at anything and everything. Someone who shows up at the stock exchange in search of that dream may be ignoring a better way to understand themselves, one that would lead them to fields where success and money would come both faster and easier.

☆　　☆　　☆

When Tom Scott and Tom First graduated from Brown University, they didn't want to enter the traditional workforce as their Ivy League classmates were doing. So they moved to Nantucket and started delivering coffee and supplies to yachts that pulled into Nantucket harbor.

When the snowy winter arrived, the yachts stopped coming and they realized they needed another source of income. Tom First remembered a peach cooler he'd tasted in Spain. Using a kitchen blender, he tried to re-create the drink himself.

What resulted was Nantucket Nectars, a multimillion-dollar business that the two have since sold to Ocean Spray.

Did making money motivate them? Yes. They knew that the yacht-servicing business was limited to the warm weather months and they had to come up with something else. But what did they actually do? Mixing the first Nantucket Nectar on a cold winter's day, recalling a taste memory from a summer vacation to Spain, is a much different experience—and motivation—from making an appearance at an office somewhere where you don't really want to be.

I couldn't wait for success...so I went ahead without it. — Jonathan Winters

To take another example.

Bill Bowerman was accepted to medical school but instead decided to become a track coach. Going back to the "color scanner" (in which Sky Blue, to the computer program, is really a combination of red, green and blue), if he had scanned both of his potential careers, what would he have learned? What "colors" or categories would have come up?

When you examine the job characteristics of doctors and coaches, you'll find many of the same categories: Practitioners in both fields are "Helpers," "Teachers," and "Advisors." In that regard, both careers he'd considered probably corresponded to who he truly was. Yet he obviously made the right choice: He was very successful, coaching in the Olympics and leading his athletes to several national titles.

Interestingly, one area where the two careers seem to be different is in the category "Science." Doctors are scientists of sorts but...coaches?

Well, one day at the track he noticed how heavy all of the running shoes were. He went home, and like a mad chemist he poured a rubber compound into his wife's waffle iron. What came out were the soles for the first, lightweight "waffle" shoes.

Some time later, he and one of his runners, Phillip Knight, put up five hundred dollars each to start a footwear company, intending to bring lighter-weight running shoes to the world.

They named their company after a Greek god.
Nike.

The key to success isn't much good until one
discovers the right lock to insert it in.
— Chinese epigram

Money II: Your Inner Synergy
1+1+1+1=You

A friend of mine is the head of a large advertising agency. She said that when she interviews people, the biggest factor influencing who she hires for entry-level jobs is neither where they went to school, their degrees, nor any of their other qualifications. An impressive resume can get them an interview, but not the job. Her hiring is based simply on the candidate's attitude and excitement about advertising.

"I don't care what they know about advertising," she explained. "I can teach them all of that. But the excitement can't be taught."

This illustrates an important aspect of the career question. It might be possible to convince my friend that you're excited when you're not, but you'll find it much harder to convince yourself of that for long.

Inner desire is key.

*To know when one's self is interested is the
first condition of interesting other people.*
— *Walter Pater*

This brings in an essential element of the puzzle:
The law of synergy. It suggests that on levels of
energy, 1+1+1+1=more than 4. Maybe 5. Maybe 10—
or higher or lower—but more than 4.

You can see this in many areas. If four people are
in a band and they click, the quality of the music they
produce is more than four times what any one of
them could have done on their own. It creates a whole
greater than the sum of its parts, a new dynamic that
is stronger than traditional logic and math would suggest. In cooking, if a gifted chef puts four ingredients
into a soup, the finished product will taste like its own
creation rather than a simple merging of the four
ingredients.

The same applies here. On a tip-of-the-iceberg
level, the level encompassing the visible part of the
world we all see and understand, my friend hires
based on people's energy. But not energy in the sense
of "look-how-many-cups-of-coffee-I-can-drink-before
the-interview"energy, but instead, the kind of energy
that's based on knowing who they are in relation to
the job.

On a deeper, below-the-surface level, her criterion
for judging people is whether they are operating from
an inner synergy. This doesn't mean synergy as in

1+1+1+1=more than 4-separate-parts. But synergy in the sense of one person, you, producing something much greater than the sum of your efforts.

How does it work? A force kicks in when you're operating from an inner passion and motivation. The world both inside you and around you answers your efforts with added dividends.

First, the world inside. When you're truly motivated, you gain access to deep wells of inner energy. But you can't just decide to open the floodgates. There's no universal entry code. Different things will make it happen in each of us, just as we each naturally respond to different foods, hobbies, and people.

Then there's a second aspect: the outer world. As you gain access to your own deepest energy, you pull back a response from the world around you. Think of it this way: Your energy is an invisible force, like electricity. As a force, it has magnetic properties, pulling forth a corresponding response from the "energy" surrounding it.

That's a metaphor for something that exists on another level, and which is hard to talk about in everyday language. It's the mysterious "X-factor" that makes things happen in incalculable ways—from coincidences that lighten your load, to finding you're in the right place at the right time, and doors that suddenly open.

We may affirm absolutely that nothing great in the world has been accomplished without passion. — Hegel

☆   ☆   ☆

This inner synergy is the force that creates wealth, while making it seem so easy and effortless for some people.

There are counter-beliefs to this one, anti-synergistic ideas that we all inherit. One is our society's conception of work, which is filtered down from old religious beliefs. The thinking goes like this: After school, the fun is over. Now I'm going to be a kind of slave.

But if work is a fact of life, and if your life is determined by your perspective, then the value of your work is up to you. It can be your greatest joy or your biggest nightmare.

Some people, whose primary goal is making money, work because they have to, and they dream of retiring as soon as they're able. The logic goes like this: "I'll do what I have to do, so that some day I'll be free to do what I like all the time."

Those same people would probably laugh off the religious idea that life is about suffering and then we go to heaven, where all is well. Their philosophy seems to the opposite: They want to make money so all will be well here and now, and they'll be free. But their philosophy is similar to the religious one: They're foregoing their current pleasure for the hope and expectation of what will come to them in time.

The biggest difficulty in that approach, besides cheating themselves out of the fun of the process, is, again, that doing just anything to make money can be a longer path to the very success it is designed to create.

Think of it this way: If you had the resources to retire tomorrow, you'd still need something meaningful to do. That is, if you wanted to be happy. Because life needs to have personal value if it's going to be interesting and entertaining. So based on the human condition, the problem remains the same.

To put it differently, you may find justification for doing work that you find meaningless. But with the justification, in the process, you'd be reinforcing a belief in a career journey that's empty. And since work takes so much of your time, the belief would lead you to a life that's hollow for you.

Yet your ability to create success comes from making life real on some level. You can do this through finding the areas that activate your energy and your personality.

☆ ☆ ☆

Finally, I'd like to talk about Bill Gates. We don't tend to think of his motivations as often as his huge bank account. But for a moment, let's look at the grandfather of information technology and who he really is.

When Bill Gates was growing up, personal computers didn't exist. Instead, large mainframe computers, the size of small cars, were owned solely by the government and corporations—and they were props you saw on TV shows or in James Bond movies.

People used typewriters. There were no faxes, but offices had Morse Code-like Telex machines that transmitted information through the phone lines.

As for the Internet, it was an emergency communications strategy for the military. The technology was slowly filtering down to some university science departments, but few people knew what it would one day become.

Gates went to Harvard, but soon heard of a company in Albuquerque, MITS (Micro Instrumentation and Telemetry Systems) that had assembled the first personal computer, the Altair. But MITS didn't have an operating system or any software. So the Altair was little more than a circuit-filled electrical box.

Gates dropped out of Harvard, moved to Albuquerque, and founded Microsoft (then known as Micro-soft), to design operating systems for the Altair.

This is a letter he published in Computer Notes magazine in 1976.

It is addressed to "hobbyists" because, at the time, the only people who knew anything about this new phenomenon of personal computers were those who experimented with the Altair—or their own makeshift "electrical boxes"—in their garages, as a hobby.

AN OPEN LETTER TO HOBBYISTS

To me, the most crucial thing in the hobby market right now is the lack of good software courses, books, and software itself. Without good software and an owner who understands programming, a hobby computer is wasted. Will quality software be written for the hobby market?

Almost a year ago, Paul Allen and myself, expecting the hobby market to expand, hired Monte Davidoff and developed Altair BASIC. Though the initial work took only two months, the three of us have spent most of the last year documenting, improving, and adding features to BASIC. Now we have 4k, 8k, EXTENDED, ROM, and DISK BASIC. The value of the computer time we have used exceeds $40,000.

The feedback we have gotten from the hundreds of people who say they are using BASIC has all been positive. Two surprising things are apparent, however: 1) Most of these "users" never bought BASIC (less than 10% of Altair owners have bought BASIC) and 2) *The amount of royalties we have received from sales to hobbyists makes the time spent on Altair BASIC worth less than $2 an hour.*

Why is this? As the majority of hobbyists must be aware, most of you steal your software. Hardware must be paid for, but software is something to share. Who cares if the people who worked on it get paid?

Is this fair? One thing you don't do by stealing software is get back at MITS for some problem you may have had. MITS doesn't make money selling software. *The royalty paid to us, the manual, the tape, and the overhead make it a break-even operation. One thing you do do is prevent good software from being written. Who can afford to do professional work for nothing? What hobbyist can put 3-man years into programming, finding all bugs, documenting his product and distribute for free?* The fact is, no one besides us has invested a lot of money in hobby software. We have written 6800 BASIC, and are writing 8080 APL and 6800 APL but there is very little incentive to make this software available to hobbyists.

Most directly, the thing you do is theft.

What about the guys who resell Altair BASIC, aren't they making money on hobby software? Yes, but those who have been reported to us may lose in the end. They are the ones who give hobbyists a bad name and should be kicked out of any club meeting they show up at.

I would appreciate letters from any who wants to pay up, or has a suggestion or comment. Nothing would please me more than being able to hire ten programmers and deluge the hobby market with good software. (italics mine)

Bill Gates
General Partner
Micro-soft
1180 Avarado SE #114
Albuquerque, NM 87108

He wrote the letter to say that he wanted to get paid. But underlying the request was the simple fact that he had been doing the work for a long time...for free.

His primary motivation was his excitement and passion for programming.

For some, moving to Nantucket or dropping everything and moving to Albuquerque on a moment's notice may be unrealistic, but the greater point remains: There are areas that will spark your interest and that sparked Gates' years before anyone had ever heard of him. That spark was where the insights and inspiration came from. Further, the quality of energy that inspired Microsoft and made it a success is the same kind of energy for something as everyday as feeling good about your life, or conceiving of something new and making it happen

There's an old cliché: Success is 10% innovation and 90% perspiration. But we often dream of success as a snapshot, a single moment in time. In other words, our model for success is winning the lottery, or taking our company public and making a fortune.

I have a friend whose company went public and who, in fact, made a fortune. The interesting thing about Dave is that he was doing what he had always done. The company was an Internet company and he was the head of domestic and international sales—but that was only a slight expansion of the job he'd had at the company where he worked before. His success required sustained activity during those years before he made it. And since he loved sales, it was natural for him.

To make a success of anything, more is usually required than just doing it once. You have to establish and reestablish the task over time, which of course you'd want to do anyway if it were something you truly enjoyed. You have to call forth your very private source of passion, inspiration and energy, or you'll find it difficult to make it happen or to sustain it.

The toughest thing about success is you've got to keep on being a success — Irving Berlin

The trick is figuring out areas where you can do this the fastest and easiest, as the sections below will discuss.

What is your purpose, what is your calling? What I know for sure is if you ask the question the answer will come. What I know for sure is, you have to be willing to listen for the answer. You have to get still enough to learn it and hear it and pay attention, to be fully conscious enough to see not just with your eyes but through them to the truth of who you are and what you can be. ... You know what real power is? Real power is when you are doing exactly what you are supposed to be doing the best it can be done. Authentic power. There's a surge, there's a kind of energy field that says, "I'm in my groove. I'm in my groove."
— Oprah Winfrey

Getting a Clue
When You Feel Clueless

Some people are lucky—they have strong ideas about what they want. For most others, it's something they have to figure out.

One person may feel she has to move in a career direction based on her degree. Or wonder whether to go to grad school.

Another person may think he should do what someone else suggests he do. And a third person may not have any idea of what to do at all.

With all the possible alternatives, where does the process start?

Often we start by tensing up feeling lost! But keep in mind that many people face the same dilemma—in fact, sooner or later, everyone does. It's important to approach this with the right perspective, since this is ultimately about figuring it out and, yes, even having fun.

There are definite ways to proceed. You'll get a good idea of what to do if you ask the right questions and keep the right frame of mind—but how you go about it is as important as what your answers actually are.

There is a famous story of the mathematician Poincaré. He didn't solve his geometrical theory during the hours he worked on it at his desk. The answer came to him when he was outside, stepping onto a bus.

Even if your instinct is to know exactly what to do *now,* keep in mind that answers that come from grinding it out are...ground out, forced. It's hard to trust in their ongoing value.

Instead, imagine for a moment that you're in a forest, sitting in the bushes birdwatching, and then watching some deer that happen by. If you make a sudden move in the animals' direction, they'll be off in a flash. You'll lose them. The art of getting a clue for career is developing the same type of sensitivity, but this time the one you're trying not to lose is ...yourself.

The idea is to observe yourself and see what makes you tick. But it's best to do this quietly and almost out of the corner of your eye. Why? Because looking straight on and getting too intense, the real *you* can disappear. Decoys take your place: other people's ideas for you; your "shoulds" for yourself; formulas that are working for friends that may not be best for you.

Getting into the process means finding ways to take a deep breath.

I cannot stress this enough. Why? Because your life is going to unfold over time, anyway. The best answers don't usually offer themselves up on silver platters. They come when they're good and ready, on their own schedule, not ours. Imagine that those answers are guarded by a master combination lock with your name on it, and they're waiting for a few tumblers of your time and experience to fall into place before they reveal themselves.

Of course, it's easy to get frustrated or angry at how slow the answers are to arrive, but the most productive thing you can do is to just prepare yourself for when they do.

An opening step in that process of preparation involves considering certain questions that I will ask below. Holding them in mind attracts answers like honey attracts flies, but the second or third answers may be best, or even the answer that comes after a month or longer.

Here's the irony: In this area, wanting an immediate answer can lead to a pressure that makes things happen *more slowly* than simply saying "I'm going to look at this as open-endedly as possible. I'll give it as much time as it takes."

Have you ever seen a straw finger trap? You put your index fingers in this cylinder and the harder you pull to get them out, the tighter it gets.

This is the same kind of thing. When you relax into the process, time suddenly becomes a strange friend. As you open yourself up to letting things happen on their own schedule, the schedule accelerates. And you can get it done much faster than you think.

So let's get started and track down what career directions are going to do it for you.

I'm going to identify three techniques to use to observe yourself. They're like three points on the same circle. Move from one to the other. When one method gets stale, shift to the next, which creates the effect, again, of the scientist leaving the laboratory and stepping onto the bus, keeping it fresh. The idea is to make the process like a song you know by heart and find yourself singing while you're thinking of something else in the street.

Try to take yourself by surprise.

Three Ways To Start
– Starting from the Trigger Questions

– What would I do for free?

– What do I think needs to be done?

– What areas of life have value and meaning for me?

– How can I be useful?

– How can I be helpful?

Take one of the Trigger Questions that appeals to you and internalize it, again, so that it comes up for you another time—for example, while you're eating or waiting for a movie to begin.

– What would I do for free?

If you think of something you'd do for free, make a mental note of it or write it down. Then stop.

Or, if you want you can take it a little further. Ask yourself: What does it involve? What are the possible categories that define it?

For example, Bill Gates programmed for free, but what was he actually doing? He was writing software. If *writing software* as a category seems to only suggest information technology, you can play with it as you might a web search. He was also *designing informational systems*. Then, to broaden it, say you take out "informational," which leaves *designing systems,* a bigger category.

The next question, Who else *designs systems?*

To think of a few: Engineers. They design everything from bridges and tunnels to electrical circuits. Who else? The question might also suggest the field of architecture.

OK. This is not the moment for the final answer. Only to make a note of those activities that you enjoy doing and, if it seems relevant, to take it a bit further.

Learn to read your own mind and everything else will come by itself. — Paul Valéry

Finally, say you ask yourself "What would I do for free?" and you come up with "I like to hang out," or "I like to go to the beach."

If you're coming up with these kinds of ideas, shift to another of the Trigger Questions or another of the techniques. But keep this in mind: There's a way to work with even *these* kinds of answers, as the methods below will cover.

☆　　☆　　☆

– What do I think needs to be done?

You'll feel energized when you satisfy what you perceive to be a real need.

Many of the answers to the question "What would I do for free?" or "What needs to be done?" will be the same. But it doesn't matter. You can work with any path that presents itself. Stay with the one that's most evocative to you at the moment.

What do you find needs action? Any political issues? Or a human service issue?

I look for what needs to be done. After all,
that is how the universe designs itself.
— R. Buckminster Fuller

Let's say I'm thinking about this and then one day, looking through a magazine, I see an add for a cruise ship and I suddenly remember that I can't stand the fact that people dump things into the ocean.

What do I do next?

Again, I keep it in mind, or better yet, I write it down. Writing down information has a certain power to activate other levels of memory and imagination, and this is true even if you never go back to read it.

So I write this in a blank book that I bought for the purpose. But two days later, waiting on line somewhere, it hits me in a flash:

"Kenneth?"

"Yes?"

"There is *no way in the world* you're going to go to the closet, get out the bathing suit, drive down to the ocean and make something happen."

I suddenly realize that though I think the oceans need to be kept clean, it's not the kind of thing that I feel inclined to do anything about.

What then?

I can feel frustrated but better yet, I can move on— finding something else that I think needs to be done, or moving to another of the questions.

You'll notice that this example didn't turn up anything definitive...yet. Difficult answers sometimes show up first, or none at all, and then it seems like the real answers will never come. But this is the nature of the process. You have to stay with it, finding time to put in small increments of energy even when it seems that nothing's happening, and then... one day you'll know what to do.

— What areas have value and meaning for me?

This is an interesting one because in a way, we all know how to answer it. There's an old saying that when we ask for advice, we already know the answer. We just don't like it!

In the same way, you know what works for you on an intuitive level, even if you've never said it out loud—just as you know what kinds of foods or movies you like.

Then why isn't this process easier? And if the goal is to find your passion, what about those people who say they don't have any passions?

I believe that the reason a person can feel passion-less is because her inner fire for career is being smothered with the wet blanket called "the shoulds," by those false ideas of how work *should* feel, or ideas of what she *should* do and what she *shouldn't*. If that same person found a way to throw off those limiting thoughts, I believe she'd start to feel not only one passion, but two or three. It's human nature.

> *Self-trust is the first secret of success.*
> *— Emerson*

Back to the Trigger Question. Let's say Lisa comes up with a great business idea that no one has ever thought of before. Her first reaction is excitement, since people succeed in business in one of two ways: by offering something new, or offering something old in a new or better way.

She's getting ready to set it up, but then she remembers one small detail: She's not at all interested in business!

In that case, Lisa would have three options.

One: Forget the idea and think of another one that will "track" for her. If she can think of one, she can think of another.

Two: Resolve to do the creative end and try to find someone else to do the business end. It worked for Calvin Klein and his partner who handled the business end, Barry Schwartz. But generally, the more levels on which you can sustain your idea, the better chance you have of making it happen.

Three is a variation of One: She can take the idea as useful input, but change it into something else by applying one of the other methods below.

– How can I be useful?

When people feel useful or helpful, they plug themselves into their own source of power and energy. If you were going to help someone or something, how would you do it?

For the most part, I do that which my own nature drives me to do. — Albert Einstein

If you were going to volunteer, what field would you choose?

If you had unlimited money to give to charities, to which charities would you give?

Don't strain. If something comes to mind, take note.

If not, move on to...

Three Ways To Start.
– Starting (or continuing) with The Detective

There's a way to proceed even before you know where you'll end up or where the path is leading.

The way to do it is to adopt the habit of seeing yourself as a detective and compiling clues and evidence.

How it works:

Let's say I don't know what to do, but I love to travel.

What can that imply?

The first answers can be frustrating. Why? The first ideas I'd probably get would be that I should become a flight attendant or a pilot.

The problem: These types of answers are too obvious. If I wanted to be a pilot, I probably would have thought of it by now.

But as a detective, knowing that I like to travel is rich with evidence. The process is subtle and I need to examine this further.

So as the detective I ask, *Why* do I like to travel?

For some people the answer may be "to meet interesting people," for others, "to see new lands and cultures." Let's say that I'm interested in meeting new people.

What does this suggest?

It suggests that I might be happier, more motivated and more successful in a career in which I deal with people rather than sitting in front of a computer. OK—if this rings true, it potentially allows me to cross many of the potential professions off the list and makes the search easier.

Or let's say I live in a small town. This evidence might suggest that I'd probably be happier in a larger town or a city, where I'd always be exposed to new people.

And if that's as far as my first investigation takes me, from "I like to travel" to "I need to move to a bigger city," I'll have solved a major piece of the puzzle. Most incredibly, "I like to travel" will have led me in a direction that didn't involve travel as a career choice ...and didn't even suggest any career at all. Yet in the process, I'll have increased my self-awareness, which in turn will get me closer to my optimum life situation.

That's the way the detective works. The more you align yourself with your ideals, the clearer your life, and in turn your career, will become.

The secret of success is making your vocation your vacation. — Mark Twain

Another example: John loves to listen to music. (John and everyone else...)

Where's the evidence in that?

If John means, "I want to sit home and listen to music" in the sense of "I don't want to work at all," the clue may be interpreted to mean "I'm tired and I need a break." The detective can take that at face value and deal with it as best he can.

But let's say he means it differently: He really wants to find a productive outlet for his love of music.

What are the first answers? The obvious ones: perform or compose music. These aren't very helpful: if he's a musician, he probably has already studied and practiced it for years. If not, the evidence may suggest taking it up as a hobby, which is important to note. But for now, let's look for secondary answers he can derive from the original information.

His inner detective asks the questions: Who else listens to music and makes a living doing it?

The answer: Deejays. Agents for record companies.

But wait. These are still obvious. And since John's a quiet, introspective person, he can't envision himself spending all day in front of a microphone as a deejay. Nor can he imagine going to smoky clubs and recruiting new bands.

But this is where he can make a creative jump. For example, he can take out the scanner and broaden his definition of music into categories to see where it leads: Music is not only sounds or notes on a page. It's also creative media. As a talent scout he would be *choosing and marketing creative media*. What parallel path does this suggest?

He has to connect the dots. What other *media* does John enjoy? He loves to read. How about a literary agency? They do the same thing with books as recording agents do with music.

The trick is to take "listening to music" into areas that may be completely unrelated to music. In John's case, once he takes it to the question "Would I like to be a literary agent?" he's heading in the right direction. If he still answers no, he needs to expand the idea further.

As you become agile enough to make similar shifts, you're on your way.

It's important to remember, once again, that one of the first requirements of being a detective is patience. You're solving a mystery. Giving yourself the luxury and benefit of the process implies giving yourself the time and the pleasure of looking at your preferences, and then seeing what directions they suggest.

☆　　☆　　☆

Now—what if I love to travel, and that information helped me learn that I'd want to move to a city, but I still don't have anything specific figured out for my career?

So I take out the blank book I stashed away in the desk and I open it. What was written there last? *Keeping the oceans clean.* I'd written it down when I was thinking about the Trigger Question of "what needed to be done."

What can I make of this evidence?

I decide to transform "keeping the oceans clean" into something else.

I think about it and I come up with the word "environment."

Obviously. Oceans are part of the environment, but is it too simple?

I take "environment" one step further. The word "parks." But just as I'm not inclined to put on my bathing suit and run down and start cleaning the oceans, I realize I don't feel inclined to do the same thing for parks in my shorts and hiking boots.

Now—I know that I'm dismissing this very fast and adopting a superficial view of the possibilities. There are definitely ways to take the idea of oceans or parks into other areas. But I suddenly get a strong feeling that I don't want to work with the natural environment at all.

Now I'm about to ask myself how I can transform "keeping the oceans clean" into "working in the *non-natural* environment". That's a big task, since oceans happen to be...outdoors.

But I'm a bit frustrated at having found no answers in this little exercise, so I decide to stay fresh and move on to the next method...

Three Ways To Start.
– Starting (or continuing) with The Verbs

Ulysses S. Grant said, "I am a verb." By that he meant that he was a person of action. Still, the most basic level of observing yourself is noticing which verbs define you and what you like to do.

There have been many systems developed for career planning which emphasize the use of action verbs in the gerund, "-ing," form to help people define their strengths. This is a very effective method, so I'll use it here.

Let's think of some famous people or professions and what they do.

Mother Theresa: The verbs: Helping. Caring. Uplifting. Feeding-Clothing-Housing, Preserving.

U.S. Presidents: Organizing, Implementing, Managing, Overseeing. The good ones: Visioning, Helping, Uplifting.

Entertainers: Singing, Acting, Dancing or whatever it may be. Amusing. ("Entertaining," but the word gives no additional information), Inspiring.

All of your actions are verbs.

Look at yourself as you live your life. What verbs describe what you love to do?

Skip stative verbs such as "to be" ("Being happy," "Being busy," etc.) and auxiliaries such as "can" and "should." Also skip verbs that don't suggest further thought. For example, "going," as in "Going to Arkansas," is not as helpful as "Exploring."

Over a period of time, playing with this idea may gradually help you attain greater perspective on yourself.

Here's an exercise that bounces you back to the Trigger Questions: Come up with one or more verbs that define why you're here. Where? Here, on the planet. What's your life about this time around?

An answer may come to mind. If not, try to come up with some in your day-to-day activities. For example, say you go out with friends. What are you "about" in that context? On the evening in question, perhaps your friend tells you her problems. During that time, you're about listening. Or maybe counseling, or empathizing, or encouraging. Those may be everyday behaviors, and they might not suggest tangible directions at first.

But a little while later, another friend joins the party. And the two of them are having a conflict and you intervene. What are you doing then? You're analyzing, or mediating, or negotiating. Does it feel good as you do it? If so, what does it suggest? If you track down a verb that describes "Why you're here," write it down and keep it in mind.

Then you go on with your life.

Let's say you like to play basketball. What is it that you like? Competing? Teamworking? Winning? Exercising? Which one?

You may find that you come up with some verbs that represent your "shoulds" even without using the word. The things you feel you *should* be about or *should* like doing, rather than the areas that represent your inner dreams. Remember, the ones that will ring true for you are those that make you feel alive.

Staying with the process will start you on your way to developing another set of eyes, those through which you start identifying the life patterns and activities that matter most to you.

Let's say you bring this in during a Trigger Question moment—say, you're doing something and thinking, "I'd do this for free."

Ask yourself, what's the verb?

Then, as you come up with verbs that describe what you like to do, or what you're "about," play with making them more specific, by extending them out into noun phrases, as I suggested before.

Back to Bill Gates (for the last time): For him, the verbs were writing and designing. The nouns were software (*writing software*)—or, adding an adjective to turn it into a more descriptive noun phrase, informational systems. (*Designing informational systems*) which became *designing systems*.

You can make it very specific, as in "designing retail systems for people who want to get inexpensive airline flights." That will suggest a specific path. If it leads to a dead end, shave off some of the words to make it more general, as you would in a web search. You can cut off "airline flights," which still leaves you with *designing retail systems* and *inexpensive*. Then shaving off "retail " and "inexpensive" opens it up again to all kinds of systems.

Make it larger or smaller as you please, and note down any phrases that catch your attention.

Daring ideas are like chessmen moved forward; they may be beaten, but they may start a winning game. — Goethe

And yet again, there it is: I suddenly remember "keeping the oceans clean."

Why don't I just forget this one? It seems to be a dead-end; a waste of time. But OK, I figure I'll give it one more consideration. With the verbs...

Keeping the oceans clean. "Keeping" is not very suggestive or descriptive. I decide I need a better word—even if it's just to put it down there, in my notebook. So I cross it out and try to think of a word that is like "keep" but more descriptive. I come up with "preserve."

I change it to "preserving the oceans."

I think, What fields does "preserving" suggest?

Antiques. That's a crazy jump, but definitely a possible one, even if it has nothing to do with the oceans.

But then I remember...I don't like antiques.

So I decide to change the verb to something else to see what comes to mind.

I come up with defending.

"Defending the oceans."

If the word "defending" sounds good to me (if it describes a piece of the puzzle, of "what I'm about"), then I'll keep it in mind to see what else it suggests.

Defending = The Law.

I could even expand it to "defending the oceans against injustice." Besides the law, what else might this suggest? Nonprofit work, or taking on companies that pollute on a grass-roots level.

If I draw a blank with all of this, I can try to expand "defending." Defending implies a type of explaining.

"Explaining the oceans." Who explains?

Teachers.

Practically speaking, would a desire to keep the oceans clean suggest a teaching career? Loosely. But "explaining the oceans" might. Or "explaining injustice."

I have to stay with whatever works and rings true—whether it's the word, the phrase, or the career it suggests. Or the question, "Am I about defending?" "Am I about explaining?"

If I write down these ideas or keep them in mind, they'll attract other ideas that expand them and make them real, like a magnet attracting iron filings. The key lies in finding the ideas that feel right—this sets the wheels in motion—and then, in trusting the process, letting your mind work on autopilot, until you come back to it once again.

Finally, know that whatever's right for you is out there. Its evidence is probably closer than you think. All you need to do is find one of many strategies to relax—to be "calmly active and actively calm," as the expression goes—and then get a glimpse of where to start.

What if you don't feel you have the time to relax and work through the process? Say you need a job to pay the bills, and you feel you can't take it slow? Then you have to do what you need to do, and take the job that seems to be the best alternative. Yet...that doesn't touch on this process at all.

There are meditation techniques that involve reciting and focusing on a special sound called a "mantra." When your mind drifts away from the mantra, you don't get mad at yourself, but as soon as you realize it's gone, you gently bring your mind back to it. In the same way, if you can keep returning to these basic questions over time, you'll be not only getting closer to answering the career question but also to knowing yourself better, which is practically the same thing.

Most Americans change careers more than once; often several times. Developing these ongoing inquiries and sensitivities as a habit, you'll insure that when the answers arrive, you'll be ready to perceive and apply them.

The Real World Steps In: Surviving Entry-Level

For many of us, starting out in a career involves heading in directions that don't feel quite right. When you're deciding whether or not to stay on a particular course, it's important to understand both yourself and the situation.

So, what happens if you have a new job and you don't like it?

This will often be the case with entry-level jobs. After all the effort it takes to complete an education, you may suddenly discover you're bored and frustrated in a position that doesn't require very much effort, let alone intelligence.

Your employers might be patient, waiting for you to find a way to make yourself useful and to learn the ropes through...osmosis. But wait a minute: Isn't osmosis the way that liquids are absorbed through membranes? Where's that at?

Obviously, only you can determine if a new situation's right for you and whether to stay or leave. But keep in mind that boredom and frustration at the start are often the doors people pass through before the job reveals a hidden layer of relevance and meaning. Don't take your initial discomfort as symbolic of the whole job—you'll likely feel better over time. And more importantly: Don't take the way you feel as symbolic of how you'll feel throughout your career. Whether in this field or another, if your goal is to find work that you enjoy and that's meaningful and worthwhile, you'll most likely find it. This position is just an opening move.

That said, and assuming you are going to stay at the entry-level job for the time being, there are ways to optimize the experience and make it easier to endure.

When you are courting a nice girl an hour seems like a second. When you sit on a red-hot cinder a second seems like an hour. That's relativity. — Albert Einstein

Let's start with a story.

I know a woman who came out of college with two passions: art and wine. She'd studied art history and her dream was to be an art dealer, but she didn't have any idea of how to get into the field. So she walked into the best wine purveyor in New York and got a job. In a few years, she climbed the ladder and became very knowledgeable about wine.

People would call her on the night of their dinner parties and ask her which wine to serve, say, with rack of lamb—and she'd tell them. It was a wine connoisseur's dream job.

She stayed at it for a while, but then she had an idea: If those people trusted her to choose a wine for their dinner parties, they'd probably trust her to choose art for their walls. It sounds like a wild connection, but people's careers are often made of such unexpected segues.

So she quit the job, began to buy contemporary art she could afford, and invited her old wine clients to her apartment "gallery." They showed up and purchased the art! Eventually, she was able to rent a space and open a real gallery. It became one of the most important contemporary art galleries in New York of its time.

Just for a moment, let's take out the "scanner" and break her situation down into its component parts. What were some of the categories that describe her position as a wine purveyor?

An Aesthetic Sense, Research and Knowledge of the Product, and Sales.

Since these same categories apply to art, it wasn't such a wild jump after all.

And that's all well and good. It holds up as a story when you look at it in retrospect, but what about how it looked at the time? What about this story from her perspective at entry-level?

During her first year at the wine company she was behind the counter, selling wine.

Which of those skills was she developing at that time?

Her aesthetic sense—learning to tell a good wine from a bad one; her research and knowledge of the product—learning the different vineyards and vintages. But even if those were the interesting parts, they were the *minor* aspects of her day-to-day life at work at the time. To put it in numbers, she might have rated the job a 15 in both of the first two categories—Aesthetic Sense, and Research and Knowledge of the Product—but in the third category, Sales, she would have given herself an 80.

Translation?

She was mostly doing one thing, sales. And what did that mean? That for the first year, she was standing behind the counter, dealing with clients. And here's the thing: that activity wasn't enough to make her feel good at work. Sales alone didn't cut it in the grand scheme of who she was, and she often felt frustrated! Not only that, but she didn't know at the time where it was leading or how well it would all turn out.

Her entry-level experience was like many people's.

Now please imagine, for a moment, a hypothetical example of an artist named Jack. Say he decides to spend a year doing nothing but studies of the ocean, So he throws away all of his paints except for the three "ocean" colors: blue, white and black.

He proceeds to make hundreds of sketches. But as the year comes to a close, he starts to feel like if he doesn't broaden the palette and get his hands on some other colors, say, some green, red and yellow, he'll definitely lose his mind. OK—but until he brings those colors back in, he'll have shut out a good many of the available possibilities in order to maximize his development on one specific track.

An expert is a person who has made all the mistakes that can be made in a very narrow field. — *Niels Bohr*

This is symbolic.

Unfortunately, in entry-level we don't usually fall into our ideal situations. The reasons are clear, the main one being that as we gain experience, we refine our idea on what those ideal situations will actually be. So what often happens is that we start out channeling ourselves into overly specific tracks, like the artist painting in only three colors, and then we move on.

How do you get through it? Find a way to make it real.

Say you're in a new job with a television news show. You have too much free time, as people often have when starting out, and you don't particularly enjoy the work.

Try to deepen your perception beyond "I don't like this," and see what's really going on.

Let's say you try to break the job down into its categories, and the two main subjects that come to mind
are Organizational Skills and Research. You give
yourself 80 in Organizational Skills and a 45 in
Research.

(And if you're not comfortable with giving yourself somewhat arbitrary numbers, these can be scored
in words, such as Organizational Skills "most of the
time," "some of the time" and "part of the time," or
to apply these to ideals, "very important," "important" and "not important.")

What do these scores tell you?

In this example, the first score, the 80 ("most of
my time") in Organizational Skills, reports that the
major part of your job seems to be keeping the office
together, pushing papers. Let's say that you couldn't
care less about organizational skills. In that case, the
score you've given yourself doesn't do you any good.
Well, think of it this way: The high mark in Organizational Skills is the symbolic representation of your
personal ticket to job hell.

But then there's the research score, representing
the information-gathering and fact-checking you do
for producers before they shoot the segments. What
about that one? Can you find one aspect of, say, a particular story that you can take further, learning more
about it and seeing where it leads?

Perhaps. But let's say you have other ideal categories that aren't even coming into play. You'd like a
flexible schedule and you don't have one. It's a competitive environment and you'd prefer if it were less
so. (I believe that we always compete against ourselves, but certain fields and companies stress

cooperation and teamwork more than others.) And there may be other categories that *do* come into play but that you don't really care about. For example, you could make a category called Politics, since in any medium-sized or large organization you'll probably getting a baseline quotient of company politics—but if you're unhappy, you may not care.

And with all of these, you might be thinking that unless something changes, you'll have to find new job or even a new field when the time is right.

But what if the time isn't right? You may need the money, not to mention that you don't know what move to make.

In that case, trust that you're supposed to find value in the experience.

How?

Sometimes it will be right in front of you and other times you'll have to create it.

For my friend in the wine business, her task at entry-level was to adopt this attitude: "I'm not particularly happy to be here behind the counter, but while I'm here, I'll wake up every morning and perform the necessary tasks—but I'll take any opportunity to learn about wine *very* seriously."

So she put herself on the lookout for wine tastings sponsored by the company; she enrolled in the wine courses they offered; she read their catalogue whenever possible, and she grilled her colleagues and even, at times, her clients about wine.

Action is the antidote to despair. — Joan Baez

How can you create meaning?

Start with where you are.

Say you're working in a large company and one day, walking down the hall, you see a pamphlet for the firm. You like the design. Ask yourself what you like about it. Who's the designer? See if the person is on staff and if you can discuss the work. Or does the company rely on an outside design firm? In that case, who's the internal liaison? Find the time to meet with that person and ask him or her about the process.

What if all your efforts lead nowhere? That's fine. The mere act of asking the question and getting the answer is the only way you'd have known. And actions lead to unintended consequences. Your activity will renew your energy and plant seeds for other activities that you'll be able to see more clearly down the road.

So look for opportunities, investigate them, and then if they don't lead anywhere, let them go.

A stopped clock is right twice a day.
— Lewis Carroll

I had an experience in creating meaning.

For many years I was in banking, but it wasn't giving me all that I needed and I felt very frustrated.

A friend had brought The American Dream Project—a mentoring program that paired executives and local middle-school students for an hour a week in the executives' offices—into several companies around the city. I decided to introduce this program to the bank.

I remember how strange yet exhilarated I felt when I walked through the door into the office of the man who would authorize it. The proposal was completely "out of the box." It wasn't job related for me at all, but of course, it soon became job-related—he was happy to sign on.

I had no trouble convincing a group of other executives to take part, and I ran the program for the remainder of my time at the bank.

"Thinking out of the box" is a big catchphrase in the corporate world and it can serve you in the context of entry-level. Consider it this way: Everything is connected...so the idea of boxes is merely a convenient illusion.

Perhaps you've heard the expression "six degrees of separation." The phrase comes from a play of the same title. It implies that all people on the planet are separated by six degrees, or six connections. (On the Internet, someone invented the "oracle" called *Six Degrees of Kevin Bacon*. You plug in any actor, perhaps actors of his generation, and the oracle connects that actor to Kevin Bacon in six steps or less.) To take this idea in a way that relates here—that every job is connected to every other job—let's call this Six Degrees of Job Relations.

To take an example: Say that Steve's in real estate. He's bored out of his mind, and he feels trapped in a box. But one day, leaving his suburban home to drive to the train station, he sees a dog-walker on the street—a woman who's walking five dogs in this affluent community. Though her job seemingly carries less prestige than his does, he's fascinated. Not only does he have a dog, but he likes animals. In fact, he'd *love* to work with animals.

But he's in real estate.

What can he do?

Is there any possible connection between dog-walking and real estate? It sounds doubtful at first, but he asks himself: What's another aspect of the service industry for dogs?"

Kennels. Kennels are...real estate for dogs.

If someone in this community goes on vacation, they'll pay a lot to leave little Chuck in his own space, like his own little apartment, in a luxury kennel. And Steve's real estate training makes him well acquainted with the business of running kennels: he understands income and expenses for property, as well as the business of charging rents, etc. The only thing he'd need to add for this animal business is...the knowledge of working with animals. But that's learnable.

How many degrees of separation was this?

Dog Walker—Kennel—Real Estate.

Starting from one end and moving to the other, it was two degrees, or two steps.

So while he was trapped in his box, he had no idea that he was actually giving himself a good education for doing something else that he'd love.

This is the spirit with which you can have faith in what you're doing—by remembering that nothing is what it seems, while always being on the lookout for the aspects of your current job that will make it real for you.

One additional activity to practice at your desk when you have the time: Keep a running list of the "scanning categories" that matter to you. Don't worry about the scores; just try to get the categories right, whether they are "working outside," "working with my hands," "having a flexible schedule," a "non-competitive environment," "working in the media," "working with ideas," and so on.

Finally, you may not find a way to be passionate day in and day out at an entry-level job. But you can try to maximize the experience.

And yes, eventually it will be time to move on. In the worst scenarios, the zeros you give yourself in all your important categories may resemble the flatline EKG of a patient in cardiac arrest.

Time to go!

Yet if you've managed to approach the experience with a measure of commitment along the way—in the sense of actively gleaning some meaning for yourself whenever possible—you'll be likely to move much closer to what you're looking for.

I'm Going to Law School (Grad School, A New Job) and I Don't Want To. Help!

Many people find themselves at a crossroads.

To go to law school or not? To go to graduate school, or to begin to find your way in the world outside? Or the question might be whether to take that job that doesn't seem quite right, or to just say no?

Obviously, the most successful lawyers are going to be the ones who love the law, and the same applies in other fields.

But what if you don't feel anything for the field, or worse, you feel a slight aversion, yet you're planning to move in that direction anyway?

This brings me to a personal story that can be helpful in this regard.

God aids him who changes. — Spanish proverb

Starting out, I always suspected I'd be happiest as a teacher or a writer, but writing takes time. And coming out of school, I didn't pursue either one.

My father always thought I should be in banking. Deep down, I knew he meant well, but it certainly didn't feel that way at the time. I was conflicted, but since I was at a point where I didn't know what to do, I took his advice.

This led to a long career in banking, in which I was moderately successful. In my view, I couldn't have been truly successful since I never really wanted to be there.

Here's the thing: I spent years in the field. So logically, you may ask if, looking back, I regret the experience.

My answer, surprisingly, is no. There are three reasons why (and I should warn you, they get progressively stranger).

First, I found a way to make the job real for me part of the time, with The American Dream Project.

Second (and with this one, I must wave goodbye to everyday logic. We don't usually think the wheels turn this way, but they often do), I had somehow absorbed from my father that banking offered one of the few "real jobs" in a "real career."

Many people are influenced, either directly or in the back of their minds, by their parents' expectations for their careers. And in my case, I would have felt like a fraud in writing or teaching. My false beliefs about "real careers" would have sabotaged me!

So...I was drawn to the job in banking. I thought it was for my father's sake, but let's face it: No one else can make us do what we don't want to do. We may think they can, and their ideas for us may trigger corresponding ideas of our own, but that's where it ends. So as I see it, I led myself to banking and in the process, I broke out of the belief that banking was the only authentic thing to do.

As I said, it took years.

Do I think it was a waste of time?

Not when considering that these kinds of beliefs can stay with us for life. We can feel like frauds *even in areas that are right for us* at twenty-five, thirty-five, or forty-five. This gives an odd meaning to the idea of "going for it," because I couldn't have really gone for anything with all my energy until I dealt with that belief.

It's funny: Back then I thought I was frustrated because I didn't want to be in banking. But I think that I was actually frustrated because I couldn't, for the life of me, understand why in the world I did!

...Could I have accomplished the same task in a less time-consuming and less painful career path? Maybe. But I didn't have any better ideas at the time.

And the final reason I'm grateful for the experience is stranger still. To put it simply, there were larger forces at work. In banking, I learned things I'd need later on.

Why is this one so strange? Because I didn't think that I was absorbing anything at all, let alone that the experience itself would be useful.

...So back to the question at hand: What if you're pulling yourself in a direction you don't really want to go?

In light of my own experience I would say a few things.

First, if you can find a good reason not to do it, then don't.

If you can think of something better to do, or you can walk away with relative peace of mind about the decision...walk away. If I'd found a good reason not to work in banking, I would have walked away. And I believe it would have been the right thing to do. I say that even knowing all I do now—the blessing it was in my life and how it freed me. Why? Because I trust that

I could have learned the same lessons in some other place and time, and perhaps even enjoyed it more and suffered less.

But what if for you, the pull is stronger, as it was for me? You don't necessarily want to make this move, but you sense that you're going to do it anyway?

In this case, I believe the best thing to do is to accept responsibility and embrace your decision.

How?

Start by respecting the inner passion.

You may ask "If I don't want to do it (if the idea alone is putting me to sleep or filling me with dread), what passion can I possibly respect?"

But let's take law school as an example. It takes an incredible amount of energy to get through it and then to pass the bar exam. Small exaggeration, but you could practically take that energy, move to Egypt and build another pyramid in your spare time. If you're going to put in that effort despite yourself, recognize that your will power is mysteriously overriding your reasons not to; overriding your very resistance itself. That's the mark of a powerful motivation and, as strange as it may seem, the mark of, yes...a passion.

It's important to remember that this alone is sure to give the experience meaning. Passions—even of this variety—yield unexpected results. You may learn something that will lead you somewhere else. Or you may work out something psychological, as I did. Or you may be leading yourself there for larger, "destiny" reasons than you can see.

Trust that when you've accomplished the given tasks, and learned the lessons you set up for yourself to learn, you'll inevitably find the next thing to do— right on schedule.

And know that these life experiences are always net gains.

The efforts which we make to escape from our destiny only serve to lead us into it.
— Emerson

Chapter Two

On Perspective

Your life is what you make it. But that doesn't mean anything until you consider this: What you make it depends on how you see it.

Perspective is everything.

Columbus discovered America.

Was he a success or a failure?

He was a failure if you take this into account: He was looking for India!

It all depends on how Columbus framed it for himself.

If the frame was "Did I find India?" he failed.

If the frame was "What did I find?" he succeeded.

As a rule, we perceive what we expect to
perceive... The unexpected is usually not
received at all. It is not seen or heard,
but ignored. Or it is misunderstood.
— Peter F. Drucker

☆   ☆   ☆

I was once in a very difficult yoga class (recommended by some extremely agile friends), and who did I see next to me one day but Madonna. In New York there are many celebrities around town, but I must say that in this case it took me a moment to catch my breath.

Part of the shock was sorting out the difference between the person and her media-driven image. What was incongruous was that she looked like just another of the women in the class, in tights. Over time, I noticed some other things. She warmed up longer than anyone else—but she's a dancer, and that shouldn't have surprised me.

In the weeks that followed, I'd see her there often and something else became obvious: her confidence. I'm not going out on a limb to state that Madonna is confident. You might take it for granted when thinking of a performer, but this was different. In that room, her confidence was palpable.

It was clear that whatever else she may have thought about herself, she knew that she was successful. And what did that mean? If she had ten movies that failed, she could still go into a movie studio and convince executives that the eleventh would succeed —because she saw herself that way.

Of course we'd expect as much: She's a successful, renowned and wealthy artist. But it's important to factor in the one thing that changes the whole equation: People who knew her in the early days—before she was famous or successful—have reported that she had the same confidence when she was just starting out and going to the dance clubs.

So, what does all this imply?

You have to "walk the walk" before the world responds. To put it another way, the most effective people are not only talented and persevering. They add one other essential ingredient: They have mastered the art of adjusting their inner frames in ways that allow them to succeed, in ways that allow them to be effective.

Success or failure is determined in your own mind. — *Paramahansa Yogananda*

The Outer Perspective: On Worry and Feeling Overwhelmed

Perspective is more a question of how you view the world than how the world actually is. Just as it doesn't matter what has happened to you in life as much as it matters how you deal with it, the art of getting what you want is the art of managing your own mind. So before going any further, I'd like to talk about worrying and feeling overwhelmed, because they are...bad management!

Worry is a form of fear, and all forms of fear produce fatigue. — *Bertrand Russell*

It's common to worry or feel a little overwhelmed after college. Your life lies ahead of you and you're not exactly sure what form it's going to take. You may listen to other people's advice, and that advice may be helpful—but the value of such advice is relative, since even *you* may feel differently about yourself in a year or so.

Whatever the specifics of your situation, you have two primary assets to create a new life for yourself: your energy and your clarity of vision. And when you worry or feel overwhelmed, they're the first to go.

Think of pilots. They're trained, when flying in a dense fog or storm, to override their visual perception and trust the guidance of their electronic instruments—rather than staring down and insisting that the bad weather clear on demand.

And now think of skiers. When they're caught in an avalanche, they're supposed to poke a hole in the snow, spit in it and see which way the spit falls—so they know if they're facing up or down. Then they have to start digging a way out...in the opposite direction!

In both of these these situations, pilots and skiers are taught to allow for their own cluelessness and shift to an alternate mode of perception.

...And ideally they all remain calm.

I'm a sports fan. I've noticed that when baseball or basketball players are interviewed before playoff games, they often make the same remark: "I want to go out there, relax and have fun."

I used to find that odd. These were the most important games in their lives. Their performances would play a big part in determining the future course of their careers. Yet they spoke as if referring to street pick-up games.

Then it dawned on me. The statement "I want to relax and have fun" carries a hidden meaning: When athletes are calm rather than nervous, they have more of their natural talents and instincts at their disposal.

The same thing applies to us.

☆   ☆   ☆

I speak from great experience. I used to worry all the time. In fact, I was very good at it.

Frankly, I thought it was a noble activity.

Why?

When I worried, I seemed to be industrious. After all, I was thinking about whatever it was over and over, so I couldn't be accused of slacking off—least of all by myself. Not only that, but my worrying implied that I was *intelligent* enough to know that there was a good reason to worry in the first place!

But I had it all wrong, as I came to realize. There was never a reason to sacrifice my energy. To say it differently, when you are in a situation that is causing you stress and anxiety, there is *always* another way to understand it.

To begin. If the way you understand a dilemma determines how easily you'll work it out, then if you're having a problem, the important question is not only "What's the problem itself?" but also, "How am I seeing it? What are the boundaries it has in my mind? Am I framing this so that there's no possible solution, and so that taking effective action will be impossible? Or can I find a way to understand this so that my perspective helps rather than hurts, and inspires rather than defeats?"

That's the goal.

Shifting Focus (Letting It Go)

When we worry we find ourselves caught in a "double bind." This psychological term describes the fate of some types of schizophrenics, who, chemically imbalanced, often see the world that way.

A classical example of a double bind is a box, and inside the box it is written:

> All Statements In This Box Are Untrue

How can you possibly deal with that?

Is the sentence true? Is it untrue? Then, is it true?

It's *impossible* to know. And if you insist on an answer, it will drive you crazy long before you figure it out.

Madness is to think too many things in
succession too fast or of one thing too
exclusively. — Voltaire

The box evokes a particularly potent form of worry: The kind where you're frustrated that a piece of the puzzle is not in place—as when you're expecting information that is going to come in a day, a week, a month, but it is still missing. A "Did I get the job?" kind of thing.

If you're demanding to know what you cannot possibly know at that moment, you're staring at the box, waiting until the moment when you'll understand the statement inside. But again, the double bind will *never* suggest a reason to stop staring.

So, if you find yourself in that situation, what can you do?

For starters, walk away from the box!

Say you look down at your watch and see that one of the hands has fallen off. What do you do?

Ask someone else if they have the time.

This shift in focus is a call to awaken your intuition, the level of perception that comes from a fresh, unfettered mind. Albert Einstein once said that intuition was our most sacred gift, and reason was merely its most trusted servant.

Do not worry about your difficulties in Mathematics. I can assure you mine are still greater. — Albert Einstein

A judge's son commits a serious crime, and the judge feels destroyed.

His colleagues ask him to take a stance. "Do you think your son is innocent or guilty?" they ask.

"Ask someone else. I don't know," he replies.

"No. We want an answer from you," they say.

"Ok..." Then he looks at them and says, "He's my son," and he walks out of the room.

As will be mentioned elsewhere in this book, there are times when you may find it strategic to think in binary terms, in yes/nos, or either/ors ("If I'm not a part of the solution, I default to being part of the problem.") Yet for perspective's sake, remember that every difficulty can have infinite solutions.

The question, then, is how do we make the shift from one point of view to another—or in this context, from one part of our minds to another?

Reframing

There's an old Chinese saying that the greatest journey begins with a single step.

This is key: Any situation that seems impossible or overwhelming can be overcome in steps that are all in scale. To say it differently: *A step you'd take to do the smallest job or to resolve the smallest problem is the same size as one you'd take to resolve the largest.*

How is that possible? Because the step can and should be no bigger than what you are able to do in the time period you are allowing yourself to do it; say, what you can accomplish in one hour, or one day.

Wisdom consists not so much of knowing what to do but knowing what to do next.
— Herbert Hoover

Let's take an example.

Say that you're frustrated about your life and career, and you define the solution to your frustration as follows:

STEP: I want to get rich.

As a motivator, that statement gives you nothing to grab onto. It doesn't suggest a plan, unless you intend to rob a bank, or run into a lucrative field such as the stock market without any idea of what to run there with. For the sake of your sanity, it needs to be reframed.

STEP: I want to find my ultimate occupation in a lucrative field.

Good, but this is still paralyzing. It can be simplified further.

STEP: I want to explore what interests me and then see how it translates into an occupation.

This involves two things, not one, so can be further changed.

STEP: I want to discover what I think is interesting to do.

And one more STEP: I will write a list of the things I like doing.

In session two, an hour later, a day later, or whenever you choose, you can take the STEP of expanding one item on the list into a new list of its own, or acting on that one item—phoning someone who might be a lead, e-mailing someone, requesting information, or going to the library.

And what if you feel exhausted after performing some of those actions...or even one? Is that crazy? No. Not if you train yourself to think of each step as a completed increment of work, and then give it a rest when you need to.

The main thing: Your smallest intelligent action can take the same effort as hours or even weeks of reactive "trying to get rich," so to speak.

And remember this: Actions yield unexpected results on levels that exist below the surface, starting, in this case, with awakening your ability to move forward.

☆　　☆　　☆

There's an old expression: Do what is in front of your hands to do. To me, this doesn't mean to simply do anything, but rather that there's always a different way of using your time and energy, especially when you're using it in ways that depress you, bore you, or drive you crazy.

Both the exercise on career reframing and the one that follows, on relationships, end with making lists. This is important, because writing a list may seem trivial and useless. You may imagine that it couldn't possibly make any difference in the grand scheme.

But shifting your perspective involves, first and foremost, shifting your energy. That doesn't mean that you need to move mountains. Thinking you have to move mountains is where the frustration and paralysis come from in the first place!

When we worry, we're like a person flooring the accelerator in a car that's sliding backwards over a cliff. Spinning our wheels, the situation gets progressively worse. On the other hand, in the right gear, a few taps on the gas pedal can be all it takes to move to higher ground.

The task of perspective involves becoming experts at tapping ourselves as we would the accelerator, at nudging our energy out of frozen patterns.

Tapping? Nudging? The real world discounts these seemingly small efforts. It measures accomplishments in terms of weight lifted and distance traveled. And when we're worrying, we tend to hold ourselves to these exaggerated standards. But to accomplish any-thing, you only need to proceed one step at a time.

If your STEP involves making a list, you're work-ing in the same vein a photographer for whom the act of taking a picture is as significant and gratifying as seeing the actual print the next day. The mere act of writing, itself, influences your energy in subtle ways.

You may refer to the list often, or you may only use it once or twice, or you may never go back to it at all—not even once. It doesn't matter. It can be an effective tool in all of these instances.

This hooks one of energy's secrets. When we get ourselves started productively, even with incremental moves, we're on our way.

Action, no matter how small, starts the process. By making a conscious move you send out a signal, just as a stone thrown into a pond inadvertently fans out rings from its center. In addition to any tangible results, you're also calling forth new ideas and inspir-ation from yourself, and you're starting bigger wheels turning in ways you can't even see.

The gain is exponential in value.

Whatever you can do, or dream you can, begin.
Boldness has genius, power, and magic in it.
— Goethe

To take another example, let's say that you're frustrated and you frame the problem as follows:

STEP: I want to get married.

That's enough to floor anyone. Talk about overwhelming? What can you do, go to the post office or supermarket, wait on line and when they ask "Anything else?" say, "Yes. I'll take a spouse, please." No. A solution will come from adjusting the perspective.

"I want to get married" can be simplified to STEP: I want to be in a serious relationship.

That is an improvement, but *serious?* No. It can make you dizzy.

What about STEP: I want to be in a relationship.

Better, but frankly, it might still paralyze. It can be taken further.

STEP: I want to meet people.

That is more manageable, but again, it's not something you can do at the supermarket or post office. Well, it is, but as anyone knows who tries to meet people in clubs, it's difficult under that kind of pressure.

To refine it further:

STEP: I want to think of *ways* to meet new people that are relevant to my lifestyle.

And STEP: I'll list these.

–Taking courses.

–Though friends.

–Volunteering.

And the next step, either immediately or in another session, is to explore the items on the list, all together or one at a time, and take action on one or more.

Or your reasoning might branch off in another direction:

STEP: I'm going to list all of the reasons *why* I want a relationship.

Then see what actions or processes materialize from that.

As long as you still have energy to keep going, take it a step further.

When you don't, shift your focus and let it go.

That's the process.

☆   ☆   ☆

How does this work in real life?

I'd like to tell a story of my own experience.

As I said, I used to be an expert at worrying. Then one day, something happened that made me see it all differently. It was a breakthrough with an ending that took me completely by surprise.

Learn to read your own mind and everything else will come by itself. — Paul Valéry

What happened...

I was looking for a job, and I thought of a friend who ran a large enterprise. I called him and made a lunch date to see him.

At the restaurant, he explained his businesses—he actually had two companies under one public holding company. When we finished lunch, he offered to hire me. He told me that he'd call and send me the package, which would include a salary and stock options. I went home, pleased and excited.

But a week passed and I didn't hear from him. In the following three weeks, I tried to call him several times but I couldn't reach him, neither in his office nor at home.

That was amazing to me. We'd had a handshake and an understanding. Even more than that, he was my friend. I assumed that if anything had gone wrong, he would have had the courtesy to call me and tell me where things stood.

As the month went by with no word from him, I became increasingly frustrated.

My worry took the form:

Oh God, I don't have the job!
Oh God, what kind of friend is this?
Oh God, he misled me!

That would have been the moment to let it go, but I couldn't.

One day it all came to a head. I knew I had to deal with it. I couldn't wait for him to make my world OK. I had to do it myself. I couldn't wait for the outside world to change. I had to change it myself.

First, I thought about my beliefs. I asked myself what beliefs I had that were causing me to worry and feel trapped. The obvious answer was that I needed the job, and that was why I was frustrated. But I knew it went even deeper on two levels.

First, as much as I hoped the job would solve my problems, I wasn't sure that it would: It was a job in the financial field, which deep down I didn't know if I really wanted. So this made me anxious for some kind of resolution. And second, there was a more personal, subtle factor: I was upset because I'd expected more from a friend. If he didn't have the job to offer, he could have called and told me.

That was it. More than anything, I was most immediately shaken that he didn't return my calls. The inner belief: The world doesn't return my calls.

"May I help you?"

"Who's this?"

"The world's assistant."

"Hello, this is Kenneth. May I speak to the world please?"

"Sorry. The world's busy right now, and can't call you back..." kind of thing.

Not only that, there was another pressing belief: My friends are not my friends. That one was harder still.

It was making me crazy. I needed to get over it, so I asked myself how I could reframe it. I posed it like this: What is one belief I can come up with that would help me with this?"

Then I realized something: I was worried about his friendship, but I could turn it around. I could think about my own friendship to him.

"OK," I thought, "If I were his friend, which I was, then what would my position be?"

I knew that as his friend

–I wouldn't hold him to something that, for whatever reason, he didn't want to do.

—I would excuse him if he were rude. And I realized that after all, his worst transgression was that he didn't return my calls, and that was merely rude. He didn't owe me anything more, such as the job. I don't believe that people are obligated to each other that way. If he acted rudely, I could let it go.

—If he had overestimated his business needs, I could understand it.

I put it all together:

—I was his friend. He didn't owe me anything. If he was rude, I could deal with it. Maybe the business had changed.

This was the first perspective shift and the first energy release. I thought that was the extent of it and in a sense, that first step was enough: The pressure was off. I felt better, free to take a deep breath and move on. Not only that, but I had renewed the friendship and was letting him off the hook. That felt good. I had handled it.

Now—that would be the end of the story, but then something strange happened, which forever changed my understanding of what worrying was really about.

It suddenly occurred to me to check the company's stock. I looked and saw that in the month during which this had taken place, the value of the stock had fallen from roughly $23 a share to $8!

I laughed at myself. It was absurd, because it seemed that logically, the situation would have worked differently. Logically, I would have *first* checked the stock, seen that it was dropping, understood why he hadn't called me back, and then I would have stopped worrying.

But I suddenly understood that when it comes to worry, the wheels turn in the opposite direction. And in my case, it was no accident that as obvious as the move seemed, I only checked the stock *after* I had found a way to let go, not before.

When we're worrying, we need to relax enough to see alternative solutions and view the situation differently. But by definition, when we worry, we're anything but relaxed! Just as our bodies slow down after eating a big meal, our minds slow down when we're overburdened with frustration and stress.

So what do we do? We keep pushing and we think, "As soon as the world gives me a reason to stop worrying, I'll stop."

Yet we need to stop worrying *first*. Then the world kicks in and reveals something new.

When I managed to let it go, I thought, "My God! Why did it take so long to see it? It was there all the time!"

It's always there all the time.

I was sorry about his business problems, but the essential thing was that by then, it didn't matter. I had made several perspective shifts and let it go.

Time eventually provided another level of confirmation as other opportunities presented themselves. The main thing: I had changed what I was telling myself and found a way to move on.

The trouble with reason is that it becomes
meaningless at the exact point where it refuses
to act. — Bernard Augustine De Voto

Part II: The Inner Perspective

It's easy enough to say that we have to change our minds and how we see the world, but it's an art— hard to do and even more challenging to sustain. Why?

It's human nature to cling to our ideas and beliefs. We defensively guard our perspective, often without realizing we're doing it. If you're telling yourself, "I want to be rich," or "I want to be married," or in my case, "When will he call back and give me the job?" and someone comes up and says, "Drop it! You're looking at it all wrong," your first reaction would most likely be, "How do *you* know?" The sum of your passion and intelligence insist that you're seeing it in the proper frame. Words to the contrary ring hollow.

This is the task of keeping perspective: understanding that our beliefs are part of us. So in addition to changing the outer frame, we're also talking about changing our deepest selves, even those parts that may be hard for us to see.

What we perceive and understand depends on
what we are. — Aldous Huxley

Madonna was a very confident person and she's highly successful.

But what if you want to be very successful but you just don't feel it?

What if, in fact, deep down you feel horrible?

Everyday logic would say, "Do it." Make yourself as successful as your dreams would allow and then you'll feel it.

There are two flaws to this approach.

For one thing, some very successful people feel horrible, so in a sense they've won the battle and lost the war. But more importantly, we're talking about no less than reversing the laws of time and space. If you can feel like a success first—before you actually create it and in the face of conflicting evidence—you'll be able to make that success happen both faster and more easily than if you don't.

Implicit in this is a key law of both perspective and energy: The changes that we think are needed in the outside world we must first affect in ourselves. Or to phrase it holistically: we're the part of the world that we need to change first. Then by the law of like attracting like, we'll attract to ourselves the fruits of that change from the world around us.

Be the change you wish to see in the world.
— Gandhi

The Oracle

This brings us into a new area: our inner landscape. To start the process, we need to have a sense of who we are.

The oracle at Delphi says "Know Yourself."

To me that seemed obvious, at first. I thought I knew myself. My identity was evident in my name, gender, nationality, hair and eye color, preferences, friends and family. But clearly, this was much too simple to be what the oracle implied.

It goes much deeper: We all have fundamental beliefs that define us, but that we don't often see them because we take them for granted. Beliefs about work: whether it's supposed to make us happy or miserable; beliefs about people: what they're really like and what they're after; beliefs about trust: who we can trust, or if we can trust at all; beliefs about what constitutes success or failure; what our strengths or weaknesses are; whether we are smart or not, or funny, or attractive.

The first step of knowing ourselves is uncovering our hidden beliefs. And then, if we don't like what we see, changing them.

Let's say Sarah has two interviews. She doesn't get hired for either job and she feels a bit disappointed, but in a day or two she's ready to move forward and begin again.

Diane also has two interviews. She doesn't get hired either, but she gets completely depressed over it and she has a tough time motivating herself to begin again.

What happened? Whatever the specifics, Sarah is relying on inner beliefs that sustain her rather than tire her out. Diane is not.

How does Diane deal with it? The normal approach is to think, "I must be crazy," or "I'm lazy," or "If I drink a triple mocha frappuccino, I'm sure I can bring myself to do it again."

Those are all external solutions, but she can also look for the answer within, according to her inner beliefs. Let's say she takes a good look at herself and realizes she doesn't believe that this career would actually be interesting. That's most of it. And then she uncovers another small piece of the puzzle: She feels overweight.

Sometimes, it's easiest to identify our beliefs by what they sound like. For Diane, it may be, "I don't even want to be here," or "This marks the beginning of my lifelong prison sentence," or "No one will possibly accept me when I'm looking like this."

Hearing and recognizing those mental tapes is half the battle. From that point, she can evaluate whether she's barking up the wrong tree by pursuing her chosen field, or not. If so, the answer won't be to go back to the same kind of interviews, but to reevaluate the careers she's looking for. Or if she doesn't believe that work itself can be interesting, she might want to find a way to convince herself of the contrary. (More on convincing ourselves later) ...And as for her perspective on her physical self, she'll need to take steps to change her appearance, or to go easier on herself— or some combination of the two.

The good news is that once she discovers the non-constructive beliefs into which she's throwing her energy, she'll start getting the energy back.

The Default

Creating your own perspective suggests that you accept responsibility for the way your life is. That's a tall order and some people may not want to go there. After all, if they're responsible for the condition of their lives, it also implies that they've attracted the bad things that have happened.

But what if someone is disabled or somehow victimized? Does a healthy perspective imply that he or she created it?

I can't answer that, but to say that I believe that signing on to the perspective game is not so much a moral or philosophical choice as it is a simple tool—for self-realization.

Here's the thing: It's hard *not* to sign on when you consider the default: If you don't actively attempt to create your own perspective, you're likely to blame the world for your present circumstances.

And then the psychological law of projection kicks in. Projection: Attributing your inner beliefs to others, or thinking that those personal beliefs represent, simply, "the way the world is."

But then that so-called *world* becomes an optical illusion. So fasten your seat belts... This is where it gets extremely strange.

The things we fear we bring to pass.
— *Elbert Hubbard*

To take an example, if my belief is "you can't trust anyone," I'll tend to think it's a fact, rather than just something I happen to believe. And what's more, I'll see myself as the exception.

Let's look at this more closely.

My Belief: You Can't Trust Anyone

– What I *Think* It Means: I, Kenneth, inhabit a world where no one can be trusted, apart from me. I'm the only trustworthy person around—which is precisely how I'm sure that no one else can be trusted.

– The Main Illusion: If I'm holding this belief, then I can be defined as "not a trusting person." Why? Because my expectations for others are that they are not trustworthy. If they're not trustworthy, who would I trust?

– The Grand Finales: There are two grand finales in this scenario. Each one is odder still.

Grand Finale #1: I'll reinforce my belief that you can't trust anyone by focusing on people who betray my trust, since they'll become my secret justifications for my belief. On the other hand, I'll downplay the occasions when someone *upholds* my trust. Why? Because those occurrences won't seem to fit, so I'll find those experiences to be random and meaningless.

It's the same with any belief.

For example, people who feel successful create that success anew everyday in their minds. It becomes an art form. They pat themselves on the back for even the smallest triumphs, since those reaffirm "the way the world is," while they discount even large failures and think "Oh, it's not such a big deal."

On the flip side, people who feel like failures will very naturally do the opposite, seeing small setbacks as huge, and seeing successes, such as promotions or awards, as insignificant.

And then, there's the final level of default.

Grand Finale #2: If I carry my belief that "you can't trust anyone," in my day-to-day life I'll be less sensitive and aware of people who might uphold my trust. What does this *really* entail? To put it simply, I'll be living in a suspicious environment.

But here's the thing: I won't be a member of that environment as a victim, or as someone who...just happened to drop by.

This is the part I'd never want to see: Like someone who has become a spy without his knowledge, I'll have turned myself into walking proof that...you can't trust anyone. I, along with others of like spirit, will be the very creators, the very linchpins of that environment—even if, to us, the belief just seemed to fall out of the sky.

A loving person lives in a loving world.
A hostile person lives in a hostile world:
Everyone you meet is your mirror.
— Ken Keyes, Jr.

*People seem not to see that their opinion of
the world is also a confession of character.*
— *Emerson*

Recording

The question then becomes this: What's the anatomy of our negative beliefs? Or, if I think "you can't trust anyone," how can I change it?

The answer is by addressing our beliefs where they live—in our minds.

I once saw Steve Martin's play "Picasso at the Lapin Agile." The story depicted an imaginary meeting between Pablo Picasso and Albert Einstein in a Paris café in 1904. Picasso was already an established artist, while Einstein was still a patent clerk.

Picasso boasted of how important he was and how his work affected the whole world. Einstein smiled and said, in so many words, his own work didn't have to affect the whole world—it only had to effect one person: Max Planck.

No one understood what Einstein meant.

He explained that to gain the kind of notoriety he wanted in the world of physics, he didn't need to please a large crowd. He only needed to present his Special Theory of Relativity to one of the few people in the world smart enough to understand it—Max Planck.

I love this image, because we all face a similar situation, as far as our beliefs are concerned.

The everyday line of thinking is that to change a belief we have to prove something to the world at large. But before proving anything to the world, we have to "walk the walk," or meet the world halfway. The solution, then, is first proving our changed belief...to ourselves.

Einstein only needed to prove himself to one person. And we only need to demonstrate our changed beliefs to the one part of our mind where it lives: in the subconscious.

To pull this off, we have to use the right language. Einstein used the language of physics, but our subconscious has its own codes for entry and operation. There are two. First, the language of imagination. Second, the language of emotion.

Let's take imagination first.

As I alluded to before, the subconscious is absurdly impartial. It couldn't care less whether the reason I believe I'm a failure is because I fell short of winning the final game in the Olympics or because I was once dumped by the woman I wanted to marry. It doesn't care whether I think I'm overweight because I'm a hundred pounds too heavy on the scale, or because I'm anorexic and I committed the sin of eating a cookie. It doesn't care whether I think I'm lazy because I never do anything and have no desire to, or if it's because I'm a hyperactive overachiever who, finally, took a day off and gave myself a break.

Whatever we imagine—true or false, absurd or not—can become a habitual belief, but how the belief gets locked in is where the second language comes in: the language of emotion.

As we go through life, our subconscious observes everything, but it only turns on its "Record" button and burns our experiences into long-term memories—and then beliefs—when we invest those experiences with emotion.

In Dante's Inferno, the lowest rung of hell was not fire, but ice. That's a good metaphor. Once a belief is burned in with the fire of emotion, it gets frozen, and then it's ours for a long time. That's all well and good when the beliefs are positive and they sustain us, but what if they're not?

Let's track the process.

We feel an emotion. This can be joy and happiness, but can just as easily be anger, frustration or humiliation. When we're moved deeply, our mind takes note. And again, the subconscious is not objective. In fact, it's even kind of stupid. I might feel worthless because of a trivial event that happened when I was a kid, but as long as I processed it with sufficient emotion at the time—say, humiliation—it registered.

Then something strange occurs. Later in life, when I receive new information that contradicts the old belief, say an award or promotion, I'll tend to treat it with my mind only—the ice of the intellect—which keeps it in a deep-chill. Yes, I might smile and try to feel good about it, but unless I permit myself to truly *feel* the accomplishment, with sufficient emotion to override the old humiliation, nothing will change. And the old belief, based on the idea that "I'm worthless," will still be in full force and effect, limiting my future potential.

*It is not enough to have opportunity; it is
essential to feel it. — Walter Bagehot*

So the question remains: How can we stop being
limited by our frozen, negative beliefs? By proving the
changed belief to ourselves, in our minds.

*Life is action and passion.
— Oliver Wendel Holmes*

Convincing Ourselves

An example. Let's say I think I'm lazy. In my
mind's eye, I'd enjoy running at the track but I never
do it. I lack the discipline.

Using everyday logic, I can ask, "How far would I
have to run to change the belief?" Since I feel bad
about myself, I'd probably exaggerate the answer, so
I'd tell myself, "Run ten miles, four times a week, for
six months."

That's a good one!

If I followed this logic, I'd probably get angry as I
suffered through it. And running and cursing, I'd very
likely hear an inner voice saying "You're so lazy...and
by the way, you're also an idiot for trying to give
yourself a heart attack." The biggest irony is that my
anger would fuel my mind and make the old system
even more ingrained. Practically speaking, the long
run would *reinforce* my belief in how lazy I was!

But what if I devised a program to appeal to the belief where it lived, in my imagination? So I cut the schedule in half, or reduced it to a quarter of the original distance, an amount that still feels like a challenge but that's clearly possible to accomplish with energy to spare.

But the new program comes with one big catch: *I have to enjoy it.*

It may sound crazy, substituting entertainment for distance. But again, in the language of the subconscious, quantity is not important. Quality is.

I could even cut it down to five laps a day, an amount modest enough to enjoy the exercise for my audience of one, my inner "Max Planck," who is the only critic I care about. But just as too many laps will make me cynical about the process, so will too few. If the number of laps is too low, I'll need to add some more. How will I know if it's too low? By my attitude. If I feel ridiculous, that's a sign to increase the count.

And of course, as the number of laps is lowered, the run may not even serve as true physical exercise. So if it's exercise I'm after, I may have to approach it separately, another time, and by the world's terms, more industriously. But the challenge here, first, is to change the inner blueprint to make the process easier.

So I begin. On the first day, I go to the track to run the laps. I have to make it real, so when I get there, I slowly stretch, smelling the grass, looking at the trees, or observing the people walking by. Then I start to run, but slowly and deliberately, so as to experience it—feeling my muscles making the effort and my heart beating.

I run the chosen distance and when I'm done, I have to make it real again. This is key: I have find a way to feel good about myself—and frankly, *that's the last thing in the world I'd want to do.* I'd more easily run an extra mile or two, or ten, as long as I don't have to enjoy it. Deep down we don't like to change our beliefs.

But running farther wouldn't be the same as taking it in. Instead, I have to walk away from that track and even manage to feel joy or exhilaration.

To make it real, I could link the changed behavior to a sensual stimulus. If I liked lemonade, I could drink one after the run as a reward, but again, *feeling it;* letting the cool taste be yet another reinforcement of the experience. Using it to tell myself, yet again, "You did it!"

And then I'd have to come back another day and start again, repeating the exercise until I knew that I'd changed the inner pattern. Some people may need to do this for weeks. For others, it may be possible to do it once or twice, with great attention.

Only you can know when you've replaced an old belief, and you'll know by how it feels.

What is now proved was once only imagined.
— William Blake

And back to Diane, who was down after not getting hired for a job. Let's say she examined her beliefs and realized that she didn't think that work itself could be interesting.

Before going back for any interviews, she could play with that limiting belief. How? By giving herself smaller tasks and responsibilities which she enjoys, and as she's doing them, convincing herself that this too is how work feels.

☆   ☆   ☆

Is this a form of tricking herself? Yes.

And back to the jogging example: Am I tricking myself?

Totally.

But another way to think of it is that I'm reversing *a bigger trick* that I came to perceive long before.

Let's say I was hypnotized by someone who poured me a glass of water and told me it was the ocean. And the hypnosis was so effective that since then, every time I pour a glass of water, I hear the roar and pounding of the surf.

It's the same with this. If I'm walking around feeling that I'm lazy, or stupid, or a loser—or I'm carrying any other belief that doesn't serve me—I'm under a similar hypnosis. Though frankly, since people usually underestimate their potential, a better analogy would be to reverse it: I'd be standing in front of the roaring, crashing ocean but believing that I was merely standing in front of a small, silent glass of water.

The task, when adjusting your perspective, is tricking yourself to correct an earlier trick, and changing the limiting illusion.

The art of being wise is the art of knowing what to overlook. — William James

☆   ☆   ☆

Of course, there's a shorter version.

Once we internalize the basic idea, we can also practice using it in smaller ways, refining the process into an everyday art form.

It's possible to make our most repetitive and mundane actions into opportunities. All that's necessary is paying attention, and remembering this basic point: The things we do absentmindedly don't make a dent in our old patterns—while the things we do consciously, invested with thought and emotion, do.

This is the art of selective attention. And let's face it, we *already* practice it, whether we know it or not. Take those people who think they're nothing despite great accomplishments. That's selective. Or a star like Madonna who knew she was a success before she actually was. That's selective as well. The only issue is whether we apply this natural instinct constructively or not.

Imagine that you say or do something to help a friend, and then you take a minute to feel what you did rather than just shrugging it off. Your action in that moment reaches down and reinforces any helpful beliefs, while at the same time refuting any lingering negative beliefs. (And this applies even if you're not exactly sure what those old beliefs are, and even if you don't remember the experiences that gave them life.) The subtle difference between truly taking in your positive experiences rather than shrugging them off may seem small on the outside, but it's fundamental.

This is not to say, of course, that you can live every moment consciously, with complete attention to every detail. But those times that you're able to feel the good things you do, your deeper self takes note, and you subtly influence who you are—and in turn, your potential.

> *There can be no transformation of darkness into light and of apathy into movement without emotion.* — *Carl Jung*

This discussion finally leads back to some simple truths: If you think that something's impossible for you to do, it will be. On the other hand, if you believe in yourself and find a way to have faith in yourself, anything's possible.

What does this mean, practically speaking? You can reframe any obstacle into something that's attainable in steps. Then, if you show up with sincerity and desire, you can override any old limiting beliefs, which will facilitate your ability to make things happen.

All that perspective asks is that you organize your world to produce and reinforce who you want to be and what you want to accomplish.

Life only demands from you the strength you possess. Only one feat is possible—not to have run away. — Dag Hammarskjöld

Vision is the art of seeing things invisible. — Jonathan Swift

Chapter Three
On Relationships

The root of the word relationships is "relate." At the beginning of this discussion, it's useful to consider this in its contrary sense: The opposite of relating is not spending some time alone. The opposite of relating is this: talking to trees and lampposts and inviting them over for dinner, and similar extremes. We're usually relating in some way, to ourselves or others, even when we don't think we are. So talking about relationships is like talking about life itself.

As far as intimate relationships are concerned, people work out different arrangements that run the gamut, from short-term fun or sex to long-term commitment—from healthy relationships with varying degrees of love and affection, to less healthy ones that seem off balance or destructive.

It's impossible to run through all of the possibilities, since there are as many kinds of relationships as there are people. But though it's hard to generalize, what I can offer is a look at some of the underlying secrets, the places where men and women get tripped up and find themselves stuck in ways that sometimes carry over into their thirties and forties. Having this information in the back of your mind can be helpful in the long run.

I hate this whole idea which is perpetuated that love is this thing that happens to you. I think you create it. You're either ready to love somebody or not. — Ethan Hawke

Getting Ready: The Step to Take

There's an expression, "When the student is ready, the teacher will appear." In the same way, when you are ready, the right relationship will appear. So all you have to do is get yourself ready.

But there are two aspects of this that are a bit more complex.

One, you attract to yourself who you are ready for—and you can always learn something from who you attract. And two, relationships are about giving. So getting yourself ready for a good one may involve, first and foremost, giving not to another but...to yourself.

This may sound selfish, but learning to give yourself what you thought you needed someone else to give you is the best preparation for a relationship—and it's a very good maintenance system once you're in one.

Years ago I would pray for a wonderful man to come and take my desperation away. Ultimately I said to myself, "Why don't you try to deal with that before he gets here?" I can't imagine any man saying to a friend, "Gee, I met a fabulous desperate woman last night."

I spent years waiting for a man to make me "feel like a real woman."...I realized that my feminine energy was not a man's gift to me but rather my gift to myself and to him...
— Marianne Williamson

So what does all this mean, practically speaking?

Let's say that Jim is lonely and he's searching for a relationship. He believes that once he finds one, he'll feel complete.

Then he meets Joanna and starts seeing her. With the onset of passion comes that magical feeling of loving and being loved. And for a while, he feels better.

But then time passes and the loneliness returns. Why? Because unless the loneliness was merely circumstantial, it's rooted inside him. It may signal an old psychological issue or an unfulfilled spiritual need.

So now Jim has a new predicament. Not only does he feel lonely, but he's in a relationship which he thought would make the loneliness disappear.

Relationships always present choices, and now he'll reach his first turning point: whether or not to recognize that the loneliness is his to deal with.

How will he choose? To the degree he expected this relationship to cure his dilemma, he'll tend to blame the relationship for not living up to "its side of the bargain."

And then what?

A few counter-productive scenarios:

1. He could end the relationship.

2. He could stay involved but have an affair, or replace his affection with a layer of disappointment or resentment—none of which would help him at all.

3. Or, a very common one: instead of blaming his partner, he might transfer the blame to himself. In this case, to "solve the problem" (in reality, to make it worse), he might try any number of compensating strategies: making himself indispensable to his partner, parenting his partner (fathering, or for a woman in a similar situation, mothering) or thinking that sex might work it out.

These scenarios could potentially add a great deal of new confusion he'd have to deal with—but then he'd be back where he started.

A faster solution would be for him to remember that whether he's in a relationship or on his own, he is the source of his own change.

This is an important point, and I'd like to stay with it for a moment. So here's another example, somewhat like the first. Let's say that Clare feels that if she had a boyfriend, all the un-together, unsettled or confused aspects of her life would fall into place.

I don't care to belong to any organization
that accepts someone like me as a member.
— Groucho Marx

She wouldn't be the only one. People often seem to carry the idea in the back of their minds that they should be in intimate relationships. Even the most independent men and women can't ignore the steady drone of a society that encourages love and marriage, including, for many women, that so-called "society" in the form of their mothers who are either subtly or impatiently waiting for them to settle down.

Despite the noise, it's important to figure out who you are and what you really want. You'll get a tip-off if you notice all the "shoulds" floating around, such as, "This relationship should be more serious than it is," or "I shouldn't be dating around and having fun but should be looking for *the one*."

These "shoulds" are generally suspect.

Personally, I waited until I was in my thirties to get married, and my wife waited that long as well. I don't think I could have possibly gotten it right before then.

I'm tempted to generalize and say that men begin to be ready in their thirties, and women somewhat earlier, but of course those types of pronouncements often fall flat. We've all known people who met in their teens or early twenties, knew they've found their life partners, and were easily able to commit. But there are just as many others who get married in their early twenties and it doesn't last.

One thing I can say for sure is that if you feel outside pressure to be involved, know that someone else's best intentions aren't going to help you make it work if you're not ready. Likewise, if you feel self-imposed pressure, remember that you'll have the clearest judgment to choose the right partner and make it work if you get involved at the right time and place for you.

And finally...some people don't choose to spend their lives with others at all. I think there are no rules in this area. If you feel you don't want to be in a committed relationship, you obviously don't have to be. And your life will certainly be less confusing if you keep that in mind.

Back to Clare. Her situation is not much different from Jim's. To the extent that she thought her life would be more together *because of* a relationship, she may turn away from her boyfriend once she finds him, feeling embarrassed, humiliated, or even resentful when she sees that her life is still the same.

She'll tend to think that he shouldn't see her this way, as "imperfect" or "un-together" because he'd lose respect. And maybe he would, depending on who she chose. Hopefully, he wouldn't. But the real problem is elsewhere. It is not that her unsettled state won't be good enough for him, but that it won't be good enough...for her.

There's an expression that if you give a man a fish, he won't be hungry for a day, but if you teach a man to fish, he won't be hungry for a lifetime. In the material world, if we get something, we have it. But in these non-material areas, if we get the so-called fish from another, we don't necessarily have it—if we put ourselves in the position of waiting for that reinforcement from someone else, we can set ourselves up to feel like losers.

We do not need and indeed will never have all the answers before we act....It is only through taking action that we can discover some of them. — Charlotte Bunch

A common variation on this theme is seeking a relationship in order to feel loved, which we all need to feel. But if we haven't mastered a degree of self-love, someone else's love will only take us but so far.

This brings up a basic point: Aspects of the human condition such as feeling unloved, un-together, insecure, fearful, frustrated, or lonely are portable. They travel and enter our relationships right along with us. And we're the only ones who can move past them.

So the solution? Knowing that in a good relationship, neither person needs to be a god for the other and solve the other's problems. All that's necessary is an awareness that each person's life itself is a work in progress.

For Clare, "getting ready" might entail considering things differently. For example, saying "I need to find some stability in my life before I even *bother* to get involved, because it's harder to do it the other way around." Or at a higher level of difficulty, if she's already in the relationship, remembering that even as she and her partner move forward, she's still the primary source of her own well-being.

Putting the Ball in Your Court

One of the biggest keys to creating a successful relationship involves seeing yourself actively rather than passively. But we're not programmed to think along those lines. It started when we were little: We all lay back and expected that someone would come into the room and take care of our survival needs. Usually they did.

As adults, we easily default to dreaming of a life partner who will materialize, come into the room of our lives, so to speak, and make everything right. But it's important to remember that we have the power to create our own relationships.

You can see when people have shifted from an active to a passive stance. But once they have, they're not always aware of how ready, or how un-ready, they really are. It comes out in their everyday attitudes and behaviors.

Each man takes the limits of his own field of vision for the limits of the world.
— Arthur Schopenhauer

For example, if a man is stereotyping and saying "All women are ____," or "All men are ____," he cannot possibly be talking down all women or all men. He can only be talking about his past and his own limited point of view.

To take a more specific example of a generalization, if a woman says "All of the good ones are taken," by her attitude she is declaring, "I'll wait here until someone comes along and proves me wrong. I have no control over this."

But since we create our lives with our own perspective, this easily becomes a self-fulfilling prophecy. What man would come into the room and prove her wrong? According to her definition, a bad one.

What is the shift that she could make?

She could give herself a greater degree of honesty and put the ball in her own court. Maybe a more truthful way to say it would be "All of the good ones...who would put up with my impossible expectations for a relationship...are taken or non-existent." Or another way, simply "I need a break. I can't put myself out there right now."

Changing from a passive to an active attitude signals a higher level of relating to herself, which precipitates a higher level of relating to others.

How many pessimists end up by desiring the things they fear in order to prove that they are right? — Robert Mallett

My wife told me that when she was single, she'd sometimes meet men who would make odd confessions on a first or second date. She said she learned to take them at their word. For example, if in the middle of a dinner one said, "I'm not a nice person," and then laughed at himself and said, "No, really. I'm not a nice person," she would make a mental note not to see him again.

His warning was a gift, and in a bizarre way, he was relating to her somewhat effectively. But since he wasn't relating very well to himself, it didn't do him any good—for as toxic as it was to say such a thing, by the psychological law of projection, he was also theoretically saying, "I'm not very nice to myself."

And he probably wouldn't have been as proud to flaunt that second statement over a good Burgundy....

Whatever he expected to come of it, what she understood was this: "Proceed at your own risk."

Let's say that unlike my wife, you're with someone who says something similarly crazy, but you're there just for laughs and you know who you're dealing with? Then it doesn't really matter.

But there's a dividing line between taking it seriously and not. Back to my wife's example. If a man says "I'm not a nice person," some may choose to go there anyway. Maybe it seems exciting, or a challenge. Or if you're not out for a big commitment, you may think he's safe, according to this questionable logic: a guy coming on with such a crazy line couldn't be asking for much time or energy. Yeah right. Whatever the reason, if you choose to travel down that road and get involved with someone who sends off these warning flares, keep in mind that people who make those kind of statements...are usually telling the truth.

The reverse equivalent of this may be the man who meets a woman who promptly informs him, "I'm trouble." Again, whether you choose to take things a step further and pursue the relationship or not, it's a good idea to give her the benefit of the doubt—and at least assume she knows what she's talking about.

> *I present myself to you in a form suitable to the relationship I wish to achieve with you.*
> — *Luigi Pirandello*

Finally, I know a man who's very critical of women, so he doesn't date very much and when he does, his relationships don't go very far. This puts him in a similar position to those who stereotype all women to be *this,* or all men to be *that.* He's defaulting to an inner voice each time and thinking, "She's not making the grade," but of course critical people are self-critical, so it doesn't start off being about "her" at all.

In the sense of "relating" I mentioned above (we are never completely unrelated until the day we're walking around talking to lampposts), you could say my friend is in a passionate discussion and, yes, *a relationship* with that inner voice. It may be a parent's, so he's unavailable because he's defaulting to the voice of his mother, who was also critical. But at best, we're only good ventriloquists in such cases. Our limitations are ultimately our own.

Now let's say he attracts a woman, but by the second date, he gets on her case. And as she storms out the door she says, "You know the problem isn't me, it's you."

And that would be the relationship. Two dates and out.

I call it a relationship, because as short as it was, there's always something to learn. (As for what *she* could learn, it may simply be that she walked away from a potentially destructive situation, affirming to herself and the world that she expects more for herself.)

As for him, there's only one movement he'd need to make, one change to enable his own growth: Going from thinking that she was the problem to knowing that the real problem was his own attitude. And if he's lucky, he'll get it.

Now—what if he had never met this woman? How long would it take him to make the same jump, left to his own devices? To go from hearing his mother's voice, or whatever it was, to knowing that he needed to change?

It could take years, or a lifetime.

Yet the two-date "relationship" will have done him a great service if he's able to understand the lesson it left floating in its wake. And in this example, the end of the relationship was potentially more valuable for his own future than the actual time he was with her.

There's a similar potential gift in all relationships, whatever their form. A later section on breakups will discuss this further.

The main thing: Whatever situation you find yourself in, you can always put the ball in your court and try to turn it into something useful. This will help you use your experience—positive or negative—to open doors to what you're seeking to bring into your life in the future.

Friendship as Model

If Barbie is so popular, why do you have to buy her friends? — Unknown

I'd like to talk about friendship, since many of the basic principles of friendship are the same as those of romantic love. But we seem to understand the principles intuitively when it comes to friendship, so much so that we take our understanding of them for granted—and we often forget to apply the same principles in this other important area.

This is interesting. Friendship is usually regarded as a kind of serious intimacy "lite." We think that if we start with the qualities that make for a good friendship and add in greater closeness and a physical attraction, we'll come out with a love relationship. Maybe so. But some people in love don't even like each other! So I think the truth of it is the other way around: If we start with an intimate relationship, and take out a lot of the junk that we throw in its way to mess it up, we end up with a good friendship.

If you can find someone you're physically attracted to for a serious relationship, and who you like as a best friend, you've hit a home run.

To begin. Sometimes we approach our most intimate relationships like accountants, keeping tabs on what we're giving and what we're getting, (asking "what's in it for me?"), while with friendship the giving and receiving flow more naturally—and again, this is a model.

To have a friend, be a friend. — *Emerson*

We trust that if we choose the right friends and we give to the relationship, we'll get back what we need. We understand that a friend doesn't take care of every need we have. Further, we may not even connect to some of our friends in certain areas, but we judge the friendship based on the whole package. This is markedly different from the perception many have for romantic relationships.

This gets into the area of giving and receiving; an area, like forgiveness, that I came to understand late in life. I learned what I know about giving and receiving through volunteering, which I've done several times.

I've found that the compelling thing about community service is this: When you set out to do it, you have no illusions about who's who. You know who's giving and who's on the receiving end. It's very clear: You're the one "coming into the room;" you're the one doing the giving—you don't volunteer to make money, by definition, and to all appearances, the person you're helping needs your assistance much more than you need to give it.

Yet I've found that I *always* received back more than I gave, and often in ways I never expected. It taught me how to conduct myself in intimate relationships, because I didn't volunteer thinking "I want this situation to give me x." Yet it always provided what I didn't even know I was looking for. It was strange. You can try it. It proves the law every time.

That's not to say that in each instance, the specific people I was working with always returned the favor. Often I received from a direction that took me completely by surprise. But this made the process even more compelling. The main thing was that the energy I put in came back multiplied.

An example. As I mentioned in the Introduction, I took part in a mentoring program for young men who had been on the streets and were living in Covenant House in New York City, trying to get their lives together. I didn't take on the assignment planning to write a book some day, and when I eventually wrote this I was thinking more of myself, when I graduated, as an example of my target audience more than the men I was meeting. Yet this book is a very important project for me, and I conceived it there.

Another example. I once volunteered at a center that gave non-medical assistance to people with life-threatening illnesses. The assistance included discussion groups and providing nutritious lunches. Mostly we were seeing people with cancer and AIDS, and somehow, it was not exactly the kind of place I expected to meet my future wife. Yet on the first day, I met a man who said he wanted me to meet his closest friend. I thought he was just being polite and I forgot about it. Over time, he and I became friends ourselves.

Two years later, he mentioned her again. And on a Saturday afternoon in July, we all got together for lunch. And six months later she and I were married.

You can of course argue that it was just a coincidence and it had nothing to do with the volunteering. But an equally sound argument can be made for synchronicity, which would form a definite connection.

Back to friendship, you may decide to give something—support, time—to a friend but notice that your efforts aren't being reciprocated. If so, you may move on, and possibly even use greater discrimination in choosing future friends. Yet we *generally* know that the energy we put into our friendships is never lost or wasted; we don't hold our breath to get the returns on a quid pro quo basis. We intuitively trust that what we put in will come back to us, and sometimes in ways we don't expect.

In more intimate relationships, we're asked to give from the heart with the same trust we extend in friendship. And if we give with sincerity, we're likely to receive back the things we didn't even know we needed.

The only interesting answers are those which destroy the questions. — Susan Sontag

☆　　☆　　☆

Another way that friendship is a model is that we don't have to be perfect for our friends and they don't have to be perfect for us. We tend to accept them for who they are. Yet in intimate relationships, not only do we sometimes expect our partners to be just right, but we expect ourselves to be. And that's a big reason why some people withhold themselves from getting involved. Not only because they might be too critical of a prospective partner, but because they may think that they're too flawed for anyone else to find appealing.

Yet in a romantic relationship, you can only start with who you are. We seem to understand "just be yourself" in the area of friendship—it's a cliché—but in romantic relationships it can be a mystery.

For example, does "be yourself" mean acting real rather than acting out of some fixed role? But what if the fixed role—say, mothering or fathering—is real for you? What then?

For example, let's say Andrew came from parents who divorced. And when he was young, he fell into the role that many children of divorce assume: feeling he had to be a parent to his parent.

Andrew might find himself doing the same thing in a relationship, and suddenly he'd be playing father to his girlfriend.

Could that be a dead-end or a rut for him? Definitely. But it could also be the opening interface through which he feels and gives love in the relationship. As I said, we all start out somewhere, and parenting is part of the human experience.

The real test will lie in whether it works for him over time. The day may come when the role's no longer serving him and he's no longer feeling what he once did. Then the question will be *Can he move beyond it?*—when the relationship comes to offer him a chance to incorporate other roles, or to let it go altogether.

> *Life is a journey, not a guided tour.*
> — *Unknown*

Another aspect of acceptance in friendship is this: We don't generally try to change our friends. If areas of their personalities are not to our liking, we tend to overlook those parts and summon our tolerance for the bigger picture of who they really are.

Yet people often try to change each other in intimate relationships.

Clearly, there are little accommodations people make when living together: women understanding that men don't generally talk and watch TV at the same time, as Dennis Miller pointed out. And men learning to lower the seat of the commode. But that's about it....

Kidding aside, people change how and when they want to. They're likely to resent any pressure to do so off their own personal schedule, as you might resent the pressure of a parent to impose on you their competing vision of who you are.

To enter a relationship thinking someone is going to change in a way they're not planning to is a waste of time and energy. Better to find someone with whom you're in greater alignment. Then the relationship will be free to run its own course, which I believe, in a good relationship, is a voyage with an unknown destination.

Don't ever take a fence down until you know why it was put up. — *Robert Frost*

The best preparation for a friendship is finding a natural connection with someone else. We often make friends with people with similar interests and experience—at school, at work, or during some shared activity. I'm sure that with most of your closest friends, you didn't have to work very hard to find them. Rather, good friendships seem to show up on their own schedule.

Applying this to more intimate relationships, we all know that it's extremely difficult to meet people, for example, in bars or clubs because those environments aren't highly contextual. Even if the bar in question draws a specific crowd, it's still anonymous. So just as the best way to meet new friends is to develop yourself and become as much as possible the person you want to be, the same applies for romantic relationships. The more you truly enjoy being yourself, the more magnetic you'll be to people of like mind, without even trying.

Taking this one step further: If you like someone and the relationship is getting serious, a good test of whether you're on the right track is whether the qualities you like in the person, beyond the physical attraction, are the same qualities you like in your friends.

What are your favorite aspects of your friends? Their sense of humor? Their loyalty? Spontaneity? Whatever those qualities may be, if the person you're attracted to possesses some or many of them, you're likely to be making a more informed choice.

Resolve to be thyself and know that he
who finds himself loses his misery.
— *Matthew Arnold*

The "C" Word: Commitment (Going With the Flow)

Many people have problems with commitment. But those problems might lessen if they realized that commitment first means committing to the process of your own growth, and your partner's, rather than committing to a specific person or the length of a relationship.

Of course, in an ideal long-term relationship, your partner is someone with whom the possibilities for mutual growth are open-ended. But until you find yourself in that kind of relationship, if you can just commit to the process, not the person, you may find it a good system to do what is right for both of you—whether the relationship lasts two days, two years, or a lifetime.

Some examples:

A woman I know told me about a man she met who she was thinking of seeing again. But she knew she wasn't ready for a long-term relationship, and at the same time, there were some warning bells going off in her head: He seemed unambitious, and though he was in his late twenties, he still lived at home with his family.

She was assessing the situation, wondering if she wanted to get involved—whether it would be fair to him and right for herself, knowing as she did that if she decided to see him, the relationship would be temporary; it would probably have an expiration date, like milk.

Of course, the question of what to do was a judgment call that only she could make. She needed to look inside herself and decide if it was a good idea or not, and then to trust the decision.

But to analyze the situation in terms of commitment, if she knew she didn't want to commit to anyone, let alone this man, would that rule out a relationship? What about committing to the process? To his growth and her own?

After all, if she thought about it and decided to get involved, it might be because deep down she knew there would be something for her to experience or learn. So the best path might be for her to live out the experience.

Part of her concern was that if she opted to see him, he might take the relationship more seriously than she did. Again, that's part of the judgment call, but in my experience, people often know the score, even when they don't consciously think they do.

Part of him might go into the relationship fantasizing that it would last forever. But simultaneously, under the surface, he would be learning his own lessons on *his* terms, and that would be the nature of his attraction to her. And of course, if she was certain that the relationship wasn't going to be long-term, she could always make that clear.

I don't think that successful relationships need to be measured in how long they last but on their own terms. One thing is sure: If you're honest with yourself and you judge that a situation's right for you at the time, you'll likely be giving to the relationship in a way that doesn't only serve yourself but also serves your partner. Being truthful to the situation is key.

Being truthful to the situation also implies trying to know what you're doing there in the first place.

Let's say that another woman, Nina, is also uninterested in a long-term relationship. She wants to get involved, but she too knows deep down it won't last. So she gets in a relationship and there's great affection, but more than anything else, it's sexual.

I think the way this works best is if she knows herself. If she's not ready for a long-term relationship, she doesn't have to put pressure on herself for it to be one.

Of course, men and women are different in this area. Like Early Man—time really flies, doesn't it?—men are biologically predisposed to see sex as sex, long before it merges with love. And as mentioned above, women often pressure themselves to expect their current relationship be "the big relationship," even if they are just out for a good time—or even if, in reality, they would never want a big relationship with their current partner at all.

Back to Nina. Let's take two scenarios.

First, let's say this relationship lasts a while but then begins to fade. This is natural. Relationships based only on sex aren't usually sexy for long. They too have expiration dates. I think this is because life always changes. Either the connection suddenly feels hollow—if you get to know someone too closely on one level, it can be hard to build a foundation on other levels—or on the other hand, the relationship wants to kick things up to another level of connection and the current level gets stale.

At that point, if the relationship breaks up when the passion's gone—and even if the love or affection remains—a sincere commitment to the process would require a respect for the relationship's need to end at the right time. In that case, if they understood it this way, they'd move on.

Let's take a second scenario.

In this one, the relationship changes as before. It isn't sexy anymore. But what if Nina doesn't want to leave? If she feels something more for her partner and she wants to stay?

If her partner's on the same wavelength, their commitment to the process will require them to shift their agenda and let go of their old ideas of what the relationship implied.

It's as if we arrive at the relationship with one idea of what it's about. For Nina, it was about having a good time. Then, down the road, we get kicked out of that garden where all was well and we're faced with a choice. And once that happens, we're unable to crawl back to where we once were. The stakes go up, allowing for either a new level of growth, or a new level of despair.

Getting kicked out of the garden means she's no longer enjoying herself. To "get back," she'd need to make the right decision. If the relationship needed to end, the best decision would be to let it end—moving on at the right time can be a loving thing to do. On the other hand, in the second scenario: if she wanted to stay but ended it anyway and went out to look for a new relationship *on the old terms,* she wouldn't feel right. Nor would she feel any better if she stayed but obsessed on why the relationship wasn't exactly as it was before.

In the second scenario, commitment to the process would entail trusting that for love to grow, it will have to include areas other than those covered by making love. Passion and compassion need to switch places, sooner or later, and then switch again. So this would ask them to stay involved and see what the relationship had in store.

In all these possible scenarios, the relationship has its own ideas for us, regardless of what we may want for ourselves. When we're willing to grow, life gives us a chance to do it.

And finally, many people eventually seek long-term relationships.

In those, we obviously commit to the person, but the essentials are the same. Life always throws us unexpected curves while giving us new chances to learn. All we need to do is let the connection take us where it will, even if it's not exactly where we thought it was going. And trust that life itself is the real process and the real thing we commit to.

The Real World Steps In: Breakups

I think that in their twenties, people usually experience breakoffs more often than breakups. Relationships come and go while people tend to focus on other aspects of their lives; rather than an ending being a matter or life or death, it's less drastic.

Yet I'd like to talk about breakups, because sooner or later, we all go through them. Further, the movement we need to make to get over a breakup is a good prototype for getting over any loss—a job ending...or even a death.

When writing in Chinese the word crisis is composed of two characters: One represents danger, the other opportunity.
— John F. Kennedy

On this subject, I'll start out speaking from personal experience....

I once had a girlfriend whom I loved, and she dumped me.

I'd like to begin with my official reaction to that experience:

Ouch.

Yet it's strange to look back.

I now see that one of the things that attracted me to her was how strong she was as a person. I didn't frame it that way at the time, but it's clear that she served as a role model for me in that area.

As I said, the relationship fell apart.

Now, years later, I believe that had the relationship worked out, I would have remained a weaker man with a stronger woman. Maybe the relationship would have had its other merits, but I don't think that one particular aspect would have changed. Just as a parent can't mold you into who they want you to be if you're not that person, a partner can't give you her qualities of character.

As I said, I suffered through the breakup. But ironically, in dealing with the pain, I gained what I never expected: I became as strong as I ever wanted to be.

Was my girlfriend able to offer this to me?

No.

Did the relationship last?

No.

Here's the thing: Was it ultimately a successful relationship?

Yes, very...but not in any way I could have imagined at the time.

Experience is a good teacher, but she sends in terrific bills. — Minna Antrim

Frankly, one of the highlights the relationship offered was the mess I had to deal with when it didn't work out. The breakup opened a door. I didn't get what I thought I wanted, but instead, I got something I didn't even know I was looking for.

Consider this: Change of any kind takes enormous energy. Think of how much pressure it takes to change a piece of coal into a diamond. In everyday life, people find it hard to access that kind of force. Yet if we're in the midst of a breakup, what does it entail? Intense frustration, disappointment, hurt and sorrow—those are all forms of intense emotional pressure; of great energy. So break-ups offer an unusual opportunity to change.

All we need to do is work it through.

The Wrong Partners, The Right Reasons

First, an observation:
People are strange.

We all are.

Let's say that Al's a jealous person.

He'll feel it if he chooses someone who's unfaithful, but he can feel it just as strongly with someone who's faithful. It isn't objective: His jealousy can call on a hundred reasons to justify its existence, or none at all.

Yet since jealousy limits his potential happiness, it will be in his best interest to change. Of course, he can choose to stay exactly as he is. It goes without saying that we're all free to be as happy or miserable as we please.

But here's the thing: Life always offers an easy way and a hard way. Obviously, we're kinder to ourselves if we choose the easy way. In this example, that would involve Al's finding someone who's faithful, and then getting help to solve his problem. But what if the movement he needs to make is too great, or he doesn't understand it clearly? If, under ordinary circumstances, he wouldn't ever do anything differently?

That is the time when, despite himself, he may take matters into his own hands. And ironically, that's why a jealous person may choose a partner who gives him *very* good reasons to be jealous. If he pushes the envelope far enough, he'll be forced to change; he'll be too upset not to.

So he may push himself to some kind of breakdown—rather than a breakup. One way or another, we all sometimes create situations to force ourselves out of our ruts. And as we're going through them, the relevant question is, "Why have I gotten myself into this? What am I supposed to learn here?"

All this is not to say that we aren't sometimes attracted to the wrong people for the wrong reasons... But in many cases it's the wrong people for the right reasons and we take ourselves, in our despair, to where we were going anyway.

> *If the only prayer you ever say in your entire*
> *life is thank you, it will be enough.*
> *— Meister Eckhardt*

Breaking Through the Two Illusions

Back to my own breakup. One day, a friend of my grandmother's noticed what I was going through. She said, "One door closes. Another opens."

I swear, I wanted to slap her (and I would have, had I been the slapping-little-old-ladies type), because even if it were true, I couldn't see it. Her advice would make sense later, but at the time, I was lost.

First, I had to get past two obstacles. One, the idea that my girlfriend didn't care about me anymore and two, that I couldn't care about her. In both cases, I believe the truth was more subtle and complex.

Let's take the first one: The person you care for doesn't care for you anymore. That is sometimes true, but not generally so. It's definitely true if you act like a crazy person at the end. It's certainly possible to turn people off.

But to paraphrase what Marianne Williamson once said on the subject of abandonment: If someone breaks up with you, all you can really assume is one thing: he or she is walking the other way. And people walk the other way for any number of reasons, some of which might not involve you as much as it may appear. She may not be ready to be involved, or she may be scared of attachment; of responsibility; of intimacy; of making a mistake; or she may just need to live her own life.

When you're going through it, it's helpful to remember that love has qualities of its own, just as the elements of air, fire, and water do. One of these qualities is its ability to transcend space and time. We all know this. It's possible to love people who have died. And if love can transcend death, it can certainly overcome the fickleness of people's personalities.

The only exception, again, is if your partner didn't feel that affection for you in the first place, in which case you wouldn't be losing anything. But otherwise, if people care for each other and they separate, the affection that was there usually remains.

The bad news is that the anger, sadness, or the desire to close the door and move on can obscure those feelings; it may take her years to remember the affection, if your partner remembers it at all.

*If people don't want to come out to the
ballpark, nobody's going to stop them.*
— *Yogi Berra*

And one more thing: Even if the affection remains, that is not to say that she will not go off and find a new partner, and maybe even feel *more* love and affection for that person.

Damn!

The love we give away is the only love we keep.
— *Elbert Hubbard*

☆   ☆   ☆

The other obstacle, after regret that our partner may not love us anymore, is this: regret that our own love for them is being cut off. But in reality, you can still love anyone. In fact, you probably don't have a choice. But needless to say, this doesn't necessarily require that they be physically present.

It's worth noting that people get tripped up in this area even while they're still *in* relationships. I know I've believed that once I loved someone, my relationship was therefore healthy. It's natural—the instinct can be to hold onto the relationship if the love or affection is real.

But if a relationship needs to end, the breakup will be easier if you remember that you can still love the people who are no longer in your life. I'd even argue that love helps the other person more from afar, "over the airwaves" so to speak, than it helps them in a relationship that has outlived its value.

But whether or not you believe this is so, the other half of the equation is much clearer: Love is a spiritual force, and the love we retain after stepping away from a relationship can take *us* places. Like the pain, the love can carry us where we didn't even know we intended to go.

Love does not cause suffering; what causes it is the sense of ownership, which is love's opposite. — Saint-Exupery

Let's look at this more closely.

When a partner leaves, you feel like you're losing a part of yourself...but you're not.

Say that when Max was with his girlfriend, he felt a certain way about life, a certain way about himself, about his potential, and so on.

Then they broke up. He misses her, sure. He wants to see her, definitely. But a large portion of his discomfort is that he lost that special feeling about *himself.* And if he doesn't feel it, he assumes that it wasn't his in the first place, but that he was merely ...borrowing it from her.

And this is the gift of the breakup: It gives him the chance to find that feeling—and once he does, it will be hard for him to lose it again.

If he felt higher levels of self-esteem, security, or contentment when he was with her, he'll have to find them again for himself. That's the task.

Those whose suffering is due to love are...their own physicians. — Proust

It is impossible for a man to be cheated by anyone but himself. — Emerson

The challenge is to reverse the perception.

...Your partner lied? ...Now the same emotions that can cause you sorrow or that can keep you angry can be employed to answer the hard question of why you believed the lies or fell for a dishonest partner.

...Your partner wasn't faithful? Then you must ask whether you could have foreseen it. And if that answer isn't forthcoming, at least you have to mourn the way you feel and practice forgiveness, so you can be peaceful about it rather than having it set you back.

...You've been abandoned? How does that affect your self-image? Can you find a way to feel good about yourself again? That's the exercise you're being given. How fast can you do it?

☆　　☆　　☆

Finally, the mentality people bring to the ending of their relationships determines what new possibilities present themselves.

Many people tend to slam the door behind them and forget the relationship as fast as possible, say, if a partner appeared to be totally off-base. But if you feel that way, you'll do yourself a service to first affirm to yourself an aspect of the relationship that brought you something, or through which you helped yourself. Figure out what self-knowledge you gained, or what lesson you learned.

That way, the experience will be less likely to leave a bad taste in your mouth, and will launch you with less baggage toward what's coming to you next.

Who we are looking for is who is looking.
— Saint Francis of Assisi

Chapter Four

On The Parents

This chapter is about you and your parents.
Oh God. Do you really have to deal with that?
Yes, you do. In a big way.
We all do.
Turning your back on this area can lead you to shoot yourself in the foot on issues that seemingly have nothing to do with your parents—and taking a quick look at these relationships can save you significant time in the long run.

Man's main task in life is to give birth to himself. — Erich Fromm

Every person's relationship with their parents is unique, but most people fall into one of three general scenarios.

Scenario #1

You just finished school and you're back home again.

You've grown accustomed to living away from your parents. And all of a sudden, voilà, your mother is peeking in your door and saying good morning, concerned about the eventuality of your breakfast. Your father is asking you when you're going to get a job, and suggesting ideas of what he thinks would be best. And you lie there...your life passing before your eyes.

It's like being Dorothy, and waking up back in Kansas.

What happened?

Was school a dream? A nightmare? Or was it somehow magically real?

Do you have a life? Or did it just disappear?

The name of the game here is boundaries. Countries are separated by borders and they develop foreign policies. Think of yourself as Russia, France, or the U.S. You need a policy, an inner template, so this situation doesn't slowly drive you to the brink of war or madness.

Scenario #2

This is a variation on Scenario #1, though in this one, you're not living at home with your parents, but your relationship is close.

For starters, if you get along with your parents, if you find that those relationships help and support you, you're lucky. Value them, because many people can't say the same.

But even if you get along, perhaps you're vaguely aware that they play too large a role in your life. Maybe you chat with them all the time, or you notice that their ideas exert a disproportionate influence on you relative to those ideas' merit. And just possibly, your mother sometimes drives you crazy, and your father remains something of a mystery.

Whatever the configuration, and even if you don't have any pressing problems with your parents, it's useful to give those relationships a quick examination to make sure that they are constructive.

There's an expression, "Under the shade of a large tree, nothing grows." So even if a parent means well and is a good role model, it's important to keep a sense of perspective about the relationships—including, in this scenario, the very human need for approval.

I fell under this category. My relationship with my parents was marked by love, but that didn't change any of the issues I had to face with them over time.

The bottom line is this: People are all different. As much as you may have in common with your parents, and you probably have a lot in common, you are unique and so are they.

It is important to consider those relationships in this light.

And...Scenario #3

You're not close to them at all. You may be angry with them, or blame them for something, or everything, from the past. You visit them infrequently or never. In fact, they may not even seem to exist for you at all.

A good part of this discussion considers parents from this perspective. Why? Because elements of this scenario apply to the others. In fact, in some ways it's easier to understand these issues when they're flagrant, while it can be harder to see them when they're more subtle.

For example, you can clearly be angry at a parent for actual physical or mental abuse that took place in the past, but you can also be angry for a reason that's harder to put your finger on—or one that is so trivial you may tend to discount it. Yet in all of these scenarios, it's best to see what's happening and to truly deal with it.

The four key elements in this chapter are blame, habitual anger, the need for approval, and how our relationships with our parents affect us in ways we don't always see. Three of the four: blame, anger, and the need for approval, are part of life itself. They can come up at work or in our intimate relationships. So it's useful to examine them in this context.

At The Lake

I once attended a weekend seminar on a lake in the mountains. We took frequent breaks, and I'd usually head outside to sit by the water. I met a young woman who was there with her mother. She attended a few lectures, but mostly she just swam in the lake or sat by the shore.

She told me that her parents were divorced. She explained that she didn't see her father and "didn't deal with him anymore."

Over the course of the weekend, we spoke every day. She always brought up her father and each time she said the same thing.

Finally, at our last meeting, I said, "You know, you *do* deal with him."

"What do you mean?" she asked.

"You've made him a part of all of our conversations."

As long as you don't forgive, who and whatever it is will occupy rent-free space in your mind. — Isabelle Holland

It gets very simple: If we don't deal effectively with our parents, we run the danger of having to deal with them anyway, but ineffectively and...all the time.

I think she had to forgive her father. But I don't mean forgiving him in the sense of approving of whatever he did, or of regarding him as a model father if he wasn't, or of liking him if she didn't—or most importantly, in the sense of making him part of her life. She didn't need to see him at all if she didn't want to.

But she needed to forgive him in the sense of reaching a more constructive understanding of the past, for the sake of finding her own inner freedom and peace of mind.

It wasn't until I was in my mid-thirties that I began to understand why forgiveness is a central tenet in many religions. Up to that time, if someone wronged me, I tended to lose my trust in the person and the relationship.

Then any forgiveness I managed was merely a way to somehow show all concerned how great a guy I was. My attitude was "OK. I forgive you," but I was vaguely thinking, "You owe me one." I kept an inner scorecard of the offense without seeing how difficult scorecards were.

Later, I came to understand it differently.

I believe that the reason to forgive is obviously not to assign the other person any guilt. And forgiveness isn't even about letting the other person off the hook, even if that's the implicit by-product.

I think that the true motivation to forgive is a more selfish one: Forgiveness is life's primary method for letting *ourselves* off the hook. It is the only way to move beyond the past. To let it go.

The girl on the lake needed to forgive her father if she wanted, truly, not to deal with him anymore. And if she couldn't forgive him, she needed to forgive the behavior or the offense, which amounts to the same thing.

Again, I think this applies to life in general but "the parents" are a good way to talk about it. If our personality type is such that we tend to hold anger, or blame people, or need approval in an unrealistic way, we'll probably start with these first relationships, our earliest.

The irony of the situation is that it's much harder to do nothing than it is to truly deal with it. And even if you decide that forgiving a parent is in your best interest (i.e. arriving at a peaceful understanding of the situation), it can still be hard to live that forgiveness once you've made the choice.

So let's run through some of the simple strategies and reasoning behind putting these relationships—however good or bad they happen to be—in an easier and more gratifying perspective.

Blame

The art of perspective implies that the past itself can't be a problem. Only our view of it potentially is. What happened is less relevant than how we currently see it. The real question is this: Do we let it become a positive factor in our lives, or do we use it to reinforce a negative world view? Does it motivate and inspire us, or is it an obstacle in our path?

Experience is not what happens to a man. It is what a man does with what happens to him.
— Aldous Huxley

The biggest problem with blame is that it hooks us into the person we're blaming. To put it simply, the first part of holding someone responsible is…"holding" that person. When we blame, we tie ourselves to the object of the blame, and the past.

It's easy to blame our parents for many things. Why? For the same reason that people give for scaling Mount Everest: "Because it is there." Our parents are there. Even if we're not in touch, they were our first and closest relationships.

But we can move past blame. Let's assume for a moment that you are in Scenario #3. You feel hurt or anger in your gut, and it seems one of your parents is responsible. I'd like to offer several possible strategies for moving on, any one of which you may find helpful.

Possibility #1

Remember that bad behavior is usually not original. It tends to be passed down from one generation to another. For example, people who hit or are physically violent were most likely hit themselves. Though I'm no scholar of the Bible, that is what "the sins of the fathers are visited upon the sons" probably refers to.

So who's guilty and deserves blame? If you were going to haul the offending parent into a court of law, they too could theoretically blame someone else. And you may end up with a long chain leading into the past.

And as we know from Court TV, it's tricky to get anyone to accept blame when they don't want to. They can always pass the buck.

But wait a minute. ...Who is going to bring their parents to court, anyway?

Probably not you.

OK, that's a weak reason not to blame, kind of circular. Let's move on.

☆   ☆   ☆

Possibility #2

An important problem with blame, in my opinion, is that you place yourself on the wrong side of a binary equation.

Binary equations are "either/ors." Take, for example, the statement, "If you're not part of the solution, you're part of the problem." If that's true, there are only two definite sides, not three or more. You're either on one side, part of the solution, or you automatically default to the other side, becoming part of the problem.

Blame is a similar either/or. We like to think we can blame someone *and* move past a bad situation, but what if one excludes the other? What if blaming someone throws you into a similar default: zapping your creative energy and reinforcing the problem, rather than using the same energy to resolve it.

I believe this is the case: If you are holding someone else responsible for your present situation, you waste the same energy that you'd otherwise be using to move on.

When you blame others, you give up your power to change. — Douglas Adams

☆   ☆   ☆

Possibility #3

This one is the most difficult but the most gratifying possibility.

To say it plainly: It's important to look at your parents at eye level, rather than looking up. As adults, we're best off positioning ourselves as equals to our parents, and looking at them eye-to-eye.

First, let's take this from their vantage point. When we were kids, our parents treated us as if they knew more about us than we knew about ourselves—and at the time, they had a good reason. When I was two, my parents definitely knew that if I stood on the window sill and leaned out, I'd fall.

As we get older, our parents often find it hard to switch from the old mindset to the present. Time flies, and they often assume that we're still who we once were, and that they remain omniscient. So, for example, a parent may get on your case because you're not exactly who they want you to be. And that can certainly be infuriating. They're implying that you are not perfect, as *they* are defining it.

But the ironic thing is that in response, we tend to reflect the identical behavior, and this is where we have to bust ourselves. Thinking a mother or father is responsible for our problems is really another way of saying, "You were not perfect as *I'm* defining it." "...You're not who I wanted you to be, and I'm upset about that."

Of course parents sometimes behave badly. And some may find that hard to excuse. But a trick to doing that is remembering that it's the behavior that was offensive. At least, that's the most positive way to see it. Blaming the person rather than the behavior leads you to demand that they measure up to your expectations. But how could they? They already didn't.

And frankly, they had a right to construct their world according to their own perceptions, wishes, dreams, and yes, fears. Even if that included being unloving or wounded in some ways that may have affected you.

Think of friends. They occasionally mess up, and we tend to overlook it. Or sometimes things go too far and the friendship ends. But we generally don't go crazy trying to remold our friends in our own image.

Similarly, learning to understand your parents for who they are is an act of kindness and generosity to them—but more essentially, it's a great act of kindness and generosity to yourself.

Does this mean that if you let them off the hook, they'll follow suit?

Let's say that you want to improve your relationship with your father. You decide to forgive him and stop blaming him for, say, not being exactly who you wanted him to be. Does that mean that he'll do the same? That he'll stop expecting you to be who he may *still* want you to be?

Not necessarily.

And probably not right away.

And maybe never.

But the test of claiming your freedom, in this case, is to give him that courtesy, knowing that he may not be able to return the favor.

Why? Because it shows tremendous respect for yourself.

...Did your parents not accept you?

Consider this: The first thing you need to do is to accept them. And in this case, accepting them may mean accepting this: "Here is a person (or two people) who don't accept me."

Then you'll be free to move on to the more difficult task of learning to accept yourself and of finding the people who will. But by first offering this to your parents, you'll open the door to go to the next level of finding what you need.

...Were they not who you wanted them to be?

Consider that the first thing to do is to understand that you may not have been exactly who they expected you to be, either. If you're asking them to give you that space, you have to give it to them. By denying that space to them, you hook yourself into the negative past.

> *A man can fail many times, but he isn't a failure until he begins to blame somebody else.* — *John Burroughs*

Possibility #4

Blaming another person gives us a place to hide from ourselves. This one is also relevant to approval, so I will talk about it in the next section.

And finally, Possibility #5: The Destiny Card.

If someone did a number on you, there are many ways to see it. We can take the attitude "My life would have been perfect if they hadn't messed it up," or we can view it holistically, factoring in that life is never perfect and that in the sense of destiny, we get the lessons we need. In this line of thinking, the biggest question is not what lessons we receive but whether or not we learn from them.

There are spiritual writings that say we actually choose our parents—that before we're born, we consent to the parents we'll have, according to the challenges they'll present us with. I'm sure this image of choosing one's parents will work for some people, while for others it may conflict with their religious beliefs. But even if you don't believe it literally, it's interesting to consider it symbolically. The bottom line: We're all dealt the hands we're dealt. The only question is how we play them. The art of gambling: Play the hand well.

The holistic view is based on acceptance, rather than resistance, as a good first step to dealing with an issue.

So let's say Beth has a mother who competes with her and she resents her mother for that. First, she needs to look deeply into the situation and see whether it concerns her mother at all. Is she competitive herself? Her mother may be reflecting who Beth is. And if that's the case, her resentment may be hiding her frustration over her own identity.

But let's discount that possibility and take it at face value. Let's say Beth is actually seeing what's there: Her mother is competitive and Beth's not.

She could take the holistic view and consider it as follows: "This situation is going to either ruin my life or be a step on my path."

Don't oppose forces, use them. God is a verb, not a noun. — Buckminster Fuller

From this perspective, if her mother is competitive, then Beth can assume she's supposed to learn about competitive people. She'll have to work it through and come to understand it, so it doesn't interfere with her day-to-day life and she can move on. This begins with her accepting that this is the lesson she's being given.

If she believes in destiny, she can even take this one step further. Beth can assume that later in life, she'll *need* to have knowledge of competitive people under her belt. So the fact that her mother is competitive provides an opportunity to gain a skill she was intended to gain.

Nothing in life is to be feared, it is only to be understood. — Marie Curie

In all of these scenarios, letting go of blame has to do with finding your freedom.

It took me a long time to understand what freedom really involved. I used to think all that was needed was physical distance. But I now believe that an essential aspect of freedom is psychological, and concerns not getting hooked into situations you don't like.

Letting go of blame is a ticket to that inner freedom.

Approval

The search for approval affects many people, both those who are close to their parents and those who are not. It's natural to want our parents' approval, because they are often the people who know us best— or seem to.

The problem arises when we aren't getting the approval we need, and we keep pushing against the current.

There are three important aspects of approval to consider:

1. Parents aren't always able to give it to us in every area.

2. If they aren't, you have to seek it elsewhere, starting, of course, within yourself.

3. Not seeking it elsewhere can be a way of shooting yourself in the foot.

Let's start with the idea that they aren't always able to give their approval. For a moment, assume that you're a parent, and you have a kid who's physically disabled and hates sports. How hard would you push her to exert herself? Maybe hard, up to a point. Maybe not at all.

But what if your child isn't disabled and still doesn't like sports? Then how hard would you push? The answer will vary from person to person.

Now let's say you see your neighbor Henry pushing his daughter in spite of what she seems to want for herself. She's miserable. And to make things worse, Henry has a big history with sports: He almost reached the Olympics in track but he got cut. Now he's possessed and keeps pressuring her to an unreasonable degree.

What would you do?

Perhaps you'd talk to him. But let's say that when you do, judging by his face and his reaction, you realize that he's incapable of getting it. It will be the end of the world for him if his daughter doesn't pursue sports.

What would you do then? You might talk to the girl. Possibly. But keep in mind that by butting in, you'd be interfering with everyone's God-given right to mess up their own kids.

My point is this: You may very well reach a stage where your attitude would shift into some variety of "Henry's nuts when it comes to the sports thing." And you'd probably leave it alone.

Now let's turn it around. A parent is, or was, doing this to you. A parent was pushing you to play ball, or telling you that you had to date more, or that you should stay in and read more, or whatever. And your need for approval would imply that in some way, shape, or form, you're still feeling the pressure now—even if you haven't spoken to your parent in five years, and oddly, even if he or she has died. But there's a time when each of us needs to say, "That's their thing. Not mine" and let it rest. ...And then feel our energy return.

Do not do unto others as you would have them do unto you. Their tastes may not be the same.
— *George Bernard Shaw*

☆   ☆   ☆

To take another example, maybe you wanted to be an architect but your parents disapproved. They said it was a crazy profession, or whatever.

You could get upset about that, which would be a waste of your time and energy. Or you could go out and try as hard as you could to prove them wrong, but that would result in a mixed blessing. Some people use anger or rebellion as a way of motivating themselves, but anger has qualities of its own that can impede your progress.

I believe the real task involves giving a parent the respect they are unable or unwilling to give you.

In this case, even if they cannot respect my opinion of architecture, I can respect theirs.

"Excuse me, Mom, Dad? By the way, what *is* your opinion of architecture?"

"We've thought long and hard on this. Sit down and we'll tell you."

(Sitting down) "Yes?"

"Architecture is a completely absurd thing to do."

OK. They are 100% entitled to that opinion.

If I respect the opinion, that doesn't mean that I agree with it—but that I'm free from having to fight it.

The thing you have to be prepared for is that
other people don't always dream your dream.
— Linda Ronstadt

☆   ☆   ☆

What about debating it or fighting it out?

Why would you do that?

First, for the sheer pleasure of arguing.

This one is definitely your call. But my advice in this case would be...get a dog.

Second, you may want to test out the idea. It can be legitimate to explore where they stand on the subject, or even where *you* stand. You may want to see how the idea resonates with your parents, respecting their judgment. Or similarly, you might examine your own ideas on the subject by bouncing it off someone else and debating it. A parent's opinion can play a part in that exploration, so this can be a good technique for determining how seriously you want to take it.

But third, you may be arguing in order to convince your parents of something they are not inclined to believe. I want to focus on this one, for I think it's a waste of time and energy. Questions like career or choice of boyfriends or girlfriends are ultimately addressed to ourselves. We need our own approval before anyone else's, and the dilemma is this: The search for someone else's approbation can be a poor substitute for giving it to ourselves.

It quickly gets convoluted. Demanding a parent's approval that is not forthcoming becomes closely linked to the assumption, "If you don't think I can do this, I'm stuck with your limiting belief about my abilities." And this quickly leads to, "If you don't believe I can do this, I can't."

This is obviously self-defeating. And there comes a point where insisting on someone's support who can't meet the request is as unnecessary as that person attempting to persuade us to adopt his or her opposing beliefs on the same subject.

We prove what we want to prove and the real difficulty is knowing what we want to prove.
— Emile Auguste Chartier

Another aspect of approval concerns hiding from ourselves.

Let's face it: if I want to be an architect, unless I'm Howard Roark in *The Fountainhead*, I don't know whether I'll like it once I start, or I'll change my mind down the road. But the only way to find out is to move toward the goal—learn more about the field, read about it, eventually study architecture, etc. And remaining on the sidelines and waiting for someone else's endorsement can be a way of hiding from taking that next step.

Why do we get caught up in this?

Frankly, we all need support. What we truly desire is the world's support...and the first patch of "the world" we look for is often that little part that we designate "mother" and "father." It's only human. But our parents' vision of us may or may not match our own. Their understanding of who we are may lack the scope of our own self-awareness.

And when we feel the gap between their perception and our own, we may try to change their perception, mainly because it can hurt not to have that support. ...But life sometimes hurts anyway, despite our best efforts.

Here's the thing: Waiting for support from people who, for whatever reason, are not able or inclined to give it implies we are not getting that support from those who would give it freely. So there is always a need to move forward and find our peers.

What we seek we shall find. What we flee from flees from us. — Emerson

What if the approval in question is more... personal?

Say you bring someone home to introduce to your parents, and your parents don't approve of the person. Or they are even downright rude.

Assuming you know what you're doing with your choice of partner, then of course you'll deal with the situation, from negotiating to establishing the necessary boundaries. But whatever course you choose to take, it will be easier if you remember that a parent's limitations for you may be just that: *their* limitations. Not yours, unless you make them so.

☆   ☆   ☆

One final note about approval.

Parents give up varying amounts of their freedom for their children: their freedom in time, energy, finance, etc. That's a good part of what it takes to be a parent in the first place: making those sacrifices.

Needing approval in an area in which they are finding it hard to give is the equivalent of asking them to continue to parent you; asking them to continue to give you *more* of that time and energy.

By freeing a parent from the obligation to see things in a way he or she doesn't—liberating him or her from having to see things the way you do, or to be an expert on a subject they may not know—you free yourself as well.

Again, it's a generous act, as far as they are concerned. But it is even more generous to yourself.

Anger

There are two kinds of anger: circumstantial and habitual. In this section, I'll talk about the second kind, habitual anger.

As for circumstantial anger, it's important to know when you're angry at any given time. Like any other emotion, anger's our body's way of telling us what's going on. But that kind of anger is not the same as anger that's an ongoing state of being. It's the difference between "George is angry" and "George is an angry person."

The main point I'd like to make is really just common sense, though that's rarely how we see it when we're worked up and going through it. If you live in a big city, you may sometimes notice angry indigent people on the street, those who are mentally unbalanced and who walk around cursing or carrying on diatribes of their inner torment and fury. Observing them, it's very clear that they're not engaged in any kind of constructive behavior, but in a vicious cycle. It gets them nowhere and has little to do with the object of their anger. It's all about them.

There is a spiritual book I used to read years ago called *A Course in Miracles*. One passage in it reads, "We are never upset for the reason we think," and it lists what is meant by the word "upset," including "fear, worry, anxiety, and anger...." I'd like to consider this phrase but substitute only anger.

It's worth noting that anger is unique in that it's a secondary emotion. It's a *reaction* we use to override the real source of the problem—the fear or hurt that came first and lie ignored underneath. When we're angry, something else is usually going on.

So to take the new phrase: "We are never angry for the reason we think..."

This is a good one, and ideally, we're all self-aware. You are indeed fortunate if you can pinpoint the source of your anger when you're angry. And I'll leave the deeper, spiritual interpretation of the line from the book to others. But I'd like to start with the obvious: If you have a fight with someone close to you, and then you go to the supermarket and snap at someone, you're not angry "for the reason you think" at the poor Ben and Jerry's shopper who cuts you off with his metal cart. And that's key.

Now I'd like to take this one step further. If you turn out to be an angry person in life, where does it come from? There are many ways to answer the question. If you believe in past lives, you might attribute its source to one of those. But let's start with this life and assume that if you're angry, you can trace many of its roots to your perception of your parents. Why? Because the way we relate in those first relationships often establishes patterns that endure.

This gives a strange twist to the line from *A Course in Miracles*. What if your relationship with your boyfriend or girlfriend is marked by anger, but you are not angry for the reason you think? What if your partner is only the equivalent of the person with the shopping cart filled with ice cream who cut you off? This may sound far-fetched, but it's worth a look.

As I get older, I notice that many people in their forties or fifties suddenly find themselves in the position of that girl I met on the lake, but with a twist. They're surprised to notice that things they "didn't deal with" in their relationships with their parents have exerted a big influence on choices they made for their intimate relationships, though they didn't notice it at the time. More on that later.

Returning to anger. We all have decisions to make in life. To be angry people or not. To be fearful or not. And I believe that we can easily trace the choices we've made by examining our current feelings about our parents. Not the question of whether or not we like them, but whether or not we've come to understand whatever happened in a way that benefits us.

☆   ☆   ☆

I'd like to tell a personal story here, not about anger but about one of its close associates, fear.

I studied Mandarin Chinese at one point and lived on Taiwan, where I taught English. There I learned that I could obtain a visa in Hong Kong to travel alone through China, which was rare at the time. So off I went, traveling to Beijing.

If you've ever been to a country with an authoritarian government, you'll be familiar with this. Every citizen is more or less paranoid and afraid of authority. And to make a long story short, to my own surprise I inadvertently caught the general paranoia in Beijing, in the same way you might catch a cold.

Maybe it was from the man I met in the street who wanted to show me around the next day, but said that we'd have to meet at a lamppost because he'd get in trouble if I came to see him at home or at work. Maybe it was from the eight guys in the restaurant who invited me over to drink beer. When they slapped down "People's" money and asked me to find an American girl for them to sleep with, I responded in drunken, laughing Chinese that it would be no different from my offering them money for a Chinese girl. And the restaurant suddenly, mysteriously fell silent, as if I'd loudly whispered out the wrong thing at the wrong time in church. Or maybe it was stumbling out to get my rented bicycle afterwards, and a disheveled man coming up to me with his hand out. I mistook him for a homeless person, but then I realized he was the bicycle parking lot attendant, asking for the parking fee. And the fee? One Chinese fen. At the time, that was half a penny.

The point is this: Everyone was paranoid but I had taken a different and most unusual path to the general paranoia: I was a foreigner...from halfway around the world...who had studied the language. Yet once I hit Ground Zero and caught the bug, my path to getting there was unimportant.

It's the same thing with anger: Once you're living with a habitual anger, say, towards your parents, the parents don't matter anymore. You've entered a new country. And how you got there—whether you were born angry, or you imagined they did something that they didn't actually do, or they really did it—is irrelevant. You're harming yourself more than you could possibly be harming them.

Once you cross the border into that new world, new laws apply. For example, when you're angry, it changes you physiologically. Your arteries constrict, your heart speeds up, and you breathe faster. If you believe, as many do, that intuition comes from a deep, relaxed place, you're cut off from your own intuition, from your own inner guidance.

Forgiveness is the economy of the heart... It saves the expense of anger... — Hannah More

But the worst part of anger is something else: Like blame, it marries you to its source. You will not stay angry *and* break free of its object, because the state of anger depends on that bondage.

I touched on this before but I would like to talk about it here in more detail.

I was once counseling a guy whose foster father had beaten him. Now it was years later and he was grown. But he had a fantasy of going back to the foster father's house, breaking in, and assaulting him.

What he didn't see is that by being caught up in the fantasy, his foster father had won...and this time, without throwing a punch.

Why? Because our biggest pitfall is not in other people's behavior but in the dynamic they teach us. Using violence as a conflict resolution technique is such a dynamic. What the guy didn't see is that by holding onto his angry fantasy, he was an "A" student in his foster father's personality type, "a chip off the old block."

The most complete revenge is not to imitate the aggressor — Marcus Aurelius

That old law 'an eye for an eye' leaves everyone blind. — Martin Luther King

As I mentioned previously, people who were hit tend to do it themselves. It passes down from one generation to the next. But here's the thing: When Victor hits his girlfriend, wife, or kids, he doesn't say, "I'm doing it because Dad did and I'm copying him." He probably doesn't take it that far, beyond thinking, "This is how you behave in relationships."

So back to this guy with his foster father. The best "revenge," the best path to liberation, would be to get over it and become someone else, rather than a copy. Strange to think that we copy what we hate, but we speak the "languages" with which we're familiar.

He needed to mourn the damage he suffered and heal himself. And in so doing, find a way to let it go and move on.

Resentment is like taking poison and waiting for the other person to die.
— Malachy McCourt

To carry a grudge is like being stung to death by one bee. — William H. Walton

Finally, some believe that anger is a good motivator. You can probably find those people who were motivated out of their own personal fury. This question is open to debate, but in my opinion, the strongest vehicle for progress is the power of your own clear judgment. On the other hand, if you're motivated by anger, at best, you might win the battle but lose the war—you might succeed as you'd wanted, but might not feel any better than you did when you started.

The best way to vanquish the anger, again, is to remember that the dynamic is a larger problem for you than the person could ever be. And the road to freedom is always the same: Forgiving. Remembering that if someone behaved badly, by definition they didn't know any better, even if they should have. The real question is how much you manifest the effects of the past you don't like, and how fast you can let it go.

The Hidden Aspects

I heard a story about a woman, Theresa, whose father, a powerful lawyer, was very domineering. She was a singer and she'd moved across the country to develop her talents, much to his dismay.

She chose a boyfriend who seemed to be the polar opposite of her father. Yet the odd thing was that he only appeared different externally—her father was a corporate lawyer and dressed like one; her boyfriend was an artist. She eventually came to realize that her boyfriend had a domineering personality and liked to call the shots, just as her father had.

I think that this is what we often tend to do, even when we don't know we're doing it. If so, there are two ways to see it. One would be to ask why she would ever be so crazy as to choose like that. The other possibility is on the destiny or holistic track: to accept that people often fall into this pattern; and then to ask how it can serve her.

Let's say that Rick's mother was an angry person and he has chosen a woman who is similar. (And of course, it can cross genders. It may have been his father who was the angry one.)

Rick may have a good subconscious reason for doing it: Maybe he wants to help her get over it, as he tried to do in vain when he was a kid with his mother; or if not to soothe, he may want to get even in some way.

Whatever the motivation, life doesn't often make it as easy as it is in the fantasy. For one thing, his girlfriend may not even see this part of her personality as a problem that needs to be resolved. And as a drama from another time and place, it theoretically has nothing to do with his girlfriend at all.

Yet if he could trace his motivation into the past, he'd realize that this is very much about him, first and foremost; not her. Then he might have an easier time accepting his girlfriend as she is, and understanding that the feelings she's triggering are an opportunity to process the old "stuff" which he may not even have known was there—and to grow.

Back to Theresa. The day may come when she'll stand up to her boyfriend, thereby helping her come to terms with her past.

But in a destiny sense, it may even go further: What if Theresa has a strong personality and in many ways she's just like her father? Maybe the only way she could have seen that was to date someone just like him. And this relationship may give her a way to activate that part of her personality—and her own journey toward self-discovery. And further, it's possible that once she meets the challenge she set up and starts asserting who she really is, she may start looking for and attracting different types of men.

My point is this: We give ourselves chances to get over the past in the form of the people we attract. And it's good to get over the past, since if we don't, we often default to those old patterns. It certainly isn't very appealing to think that a partner is similar to a parent in ways we don't like—and as a result we're not naturally predisposed to make the association. Yet it's clear that relationships are a place to work out the things we need to, and to learn.

Most people are other people. Their thoughts are someone else's opinions, their lives a mimicry, their passions a quotation.
— Oscar Wilde

The best way out is always through.
— *Helen Keller*

A "fast track" method for determining where we are with all of this, again, is to examine our relationships with our parents. When I say "examine the relationships," I'm not necessarily implying a therapeutic analysis, though that may be right for some. More immediately, you can know if you've neglected to deal with something in the past by simply examining your feelings about your parents in the present. It doesn't matter if you like them or you don't. But if you're still carrying, say, resentment, remember that the resentment can sabotage you elsewhere.

I believe the subject of the parents is like a buoy floating above a shipwreck in the middle of the ocean. When it seems that they're the problem, I think they're usually only the marker. When we peer below the surface, it becomes not the buoy we were concerned with at all, but the boat lying beneath it—those parts of ourselves that we've hidden from sight but which affect us.

Conversely, when we decide to let our parents off the hook in the present (whatever we feel about them—respecting them enough to give them the benefit of the doubt and forgive them), it's a sign that we'll have far fewer surprises popping up in our own relationships, and we're sure to have a clearer sense of what those relationships are about.

☆　☆　☆

If, by the laws of forgiveness, giving the parents a break is the only way to give oneself the same break, what would stop someone from doing it?

During the Cold War, America practiced the doctrine of M.A.D. (mutually assured destruction) with its adversary. The theory was that each side had enough nuclear weapons to wipe out the other, and that was the deterrent; an effective one, as it turned out. Yet the maxim, stated in the negative, was absurd because it essentially said, "If you destroy me, I'll destroy you back. We'll all die."

This is the same philosophy we're employing when we can't forgive. First we think, "I'm punishing the other person." The next step will be a little more realistic: "My attitude might cost me *my* peace of mind, but at least it will harm them as much, or even more." That's M.A.D. But then, if we factor in that the people we think we're punishing may not be on board with that, and may not necessarily be harmed at all, while our grudges always reflect back on ourselves, this leads to the final revision: "I'll liberate them to liberate myself."

The keenest sorrow is to recognize ourselves as the sole cause of our adversities. — Sophocles

☆　　☆　　☆

Finally, I'd like to take a moment to talk about active versus reactive choices.

Like Theresa, many people choose partners in reaction to their parents. Obviously, there are sometimes reasons to react, depending on the situation. And more generally, there are obviously times in life to rebel or dissent. But the thing to consider is this: Like anger or blame, choices made as a reaction carry the fingerprints of that which they are reacting to.

If your parents were religious conservatives and you find yourself looking for an appealing atheist, remember that if you were not in a reactive mode, your choice might be different still. If one of your parents wanted you to be a doctor and you decide to go into business, make sure you want to be in business, because you can be as unhappy in one career as the other.

This is an important dynamic: Choices made without pressure from yourself or others are going to be better choices for you. So you'll do yourself a remarkable service if, as much as possible, you develop techniques to give yourself the space to see yourself clearly, with a minimum of pressure.

And as far as your parents are concerned, this is the reason, again, for examining the issue of whether you are clear on whatever happened—and coming to a peaceful and productive understanding of the past.

To do just the opposite is also a form of imitation. — *Georg C. Lichtenberg*

Life is an adventure in forgiveness.
— *Norman Cousins*

☆ ☆ ☆

Chapter Five

On Faith In Yourself

It is important to develop your faith.

Faith in what?

In yourself, and in life and its processes.

What does faith imply? First, knowing that you do not and cannot know everything that you need to know, but that you'll know it all in time.

We perceive things as fixed but they're always changing. So there's only so much you *can* know in advance.

Trusting that things unfold right on schedule is not wishful thinking, but a strong survival strategy. It's as essential as breathing.

Nature offers many examples of faith.

Let's say you're a castaway on an island. You're surviving on little food, and all of a sudden, a woman appears and she gives you a seed.

You look at it.

Then she asks you what it is.

You say, "I don't know."

She says, "Tell me what it is right now."

You say, "Hold on! I don't know, and I'll need some time to figure it out."

Then you'd have to plant the seed and wait and see what came up. No problem there.

But what if she said something crazy like "If you don't tell me what it is right now, then I can't let you have it," or "If you don't know what it is, it doesn't exist."

What could you possibly reply?

A. "There are many good forms of therapy available for you when we return to the mainland."

B. "Thank you, I've already eaten."

Her questions are clearly out of line. But how are they different from wanting to know exactly what your career's going to be before you start? Or thinking that if you don't know what it is, then you can't possibly be on your way?

I'm not saying you don't need to come up with a working plan for your career, some sort of temporary guidance system—just so long as it's not too narrowly defined and is open to change.

But then you still need faith in information that will come to you that you can't possibly know yet. First you have to "plant the seed."

Then what's the next step?

Intelligent movement. And living out the process.

Nature offers another example of faith.

Think of a rose tree surrounded by fertilizer.
Think of the beautiful flower, the rose, and what feeds it: the cow manure.
The beauty comes out of what is not beautiful.

If that's the way things work on the planet, how is it different from knowing, in the face of a tragedy such as a death, or one as everyday as a love affair that crashes and burns, that something else will come out of it—something that isn't horrible, but which is redeeming and even beautiful?
Faith is a matter of assuming in advance that this is how it works.

And of course, if you happen to be one who finds beauty in cow manure, well, that's a subject I really can't talk about here....

I have a friend who was fired from his job. He was at a loss. Needing to do something, he went out and started his own business, which became highly successful. If you ask him, he'll tell you that he never would have become an entrepreneur if he hadn't been fired.

So the only way he would have done it is if someone had said, "Look. I know you don't want to get fired, but if it happens, you'll end up creating your own company and you'll do very well." But no one ever says this type of thing and if they did, they'd sound crazy.

As I mentioned, I was once in a relationship which ended and drove me to my own private hell. Yet I grew up as a result and it cleared the path for me to meet my wife.

What if someone had said, "She's going to dump you and it's really going to hurt. But you need to go through it and I promise you, your life will be better as a result."

What would I have said? "No, thank you."

So let's say you find yourself in a destructive relationship that ends badly. There are two ways to look at it. The first is to think it was a mistake, or tell yourself "I must have been out of my mind."

The second way is to take responsibility for it and say "This had *everything* to do with me," and then move on to the question, "What did I need to learn here?"

Let's say the lesson is "learn to respect yourself." And the way you're going to get it is to see what it's like to spend time with someone who doesn't respect you. This may sound like a long or pathetic way to learn about yourself, but relationships often teach us this way, by trial and error.

Everyone is perfectly willing to learn from
unpleasant experience—if only the damage
of the first lesson could be repaired.
— Georg C. Lichtenberg

If that's the case, what sense is there in saying, "I know exactly what my ideal partner will be like," when here you may attract a person who isn't ideal, but who's the crucible that can help you shape and understand who that ideal partner will eventually be? And further, if you don't experience this other person first, you may never move to that greater level of refinement and self-understanding that will prepare you for the partner you're dreaming of.

It's the same when it comes to your career. You may think you want one type of career, but the experience of moving forward in that direction will make another type possible.

Faith means believing that if you take the next step, while trusting yourself and keeping your eyes open, the rest will take care of itself.

Next, people have said it in a million ways...

*Problems are only opportunities in work
clothes. — Henry J. Keiser*

We often have ideas about our lives working out
perfectly. But let's talk about "perfect" for a moment:
It's not the way the wheels seem to turn in real time.
It's as if we expect the roses to somehow grow without the fertilizer.

But what if on the other hand, we trusted that our
experience was to our general benefit, and saw even
our difficulties as part of a larger plan?

I'll take it one step further. What if you trusted
that you are aided by the world around you?

That's a tricky one. It sounds like I'm saying that
the world is benevolent. With all that goes on, including wars and random evil, it may be difficult to
believe that the world's playing any kind of constructive role in your life.

But again, this is not about the world being merely
good or bad. We all inherit our own little portion of
darkness along the way, including things not working
out the way we want them to. But faith in yourself
assumes that this too is part of each person's very personal life plan.

Herbie Hancock, the celebrated jazz pianist, told a
story from when he was playing in a band with the
legendary Miles Davis. During one number, he played
a chord on the piano that was completely off-key. He

cringed and leaned away from the piano. But Miles heard it, took it in, and effortlessly played a few notes on the trumpet which somehow made Hancock's dissonant chord fit right in.

This suggests not a line but a cycle: Life sends us experiences, and we're asked to trust that whatever comes our way, we'll have an opportunity to deal with it. And in dealing with it and learning from it as best we can, we get closer to where we're already going; we advance further down the road we're already on.

In that sense, we don't need everything to work out perfectly.

We just need it to...work out.

If you can find a path with no obstacles,
it probably doesn't lead anywhere.
— Frank A. Clark

☆   ☆   ☆

An example.

As a young man, Ronald Reagan applied for a job as a manager at a Montgomery Ward department store in his home town. He didn't get the job, and his ideas about his life and future were short-circuited.

At a loss, he found a job in a completely different field, as a radio broadcaster. To his surprise, he liked it. Over time, he learned to be a skilled communictor. That led to an acting career, to heading the actors' union, and then to a job as a traveling spokesperson for General Electric. This all led to politics.

He had a similarly unpredictable path in marriage. He was humiliated by his divorce from his first wife, but his second wife was clearly the love of his life.

Reagan always said his mother had taught him that when something he wanted didn't come through, it was because something better was on its way. Since her idea sounds like a spiritual belief, it may appeal to you or it may not. (And those who didn't approve of Ronald Reagan's political agenda probably wish he'd gotten that job in the department store!) But whether or not his mother's philosophy is universally true, it was certainly effective and convenient. It enabled him to make smooth transitions on his path.

Nobody can be exactly like me. Sometimes even I have trouble doing it. — Tallulah Bankhead

Another example.

The Long March was one of the most celebrated incidents in the Chinese Revolution of 1949. One strange thing about the Long March, though: It started out as a retreat!

Mao's soldiers were overpowered outside the city of Jiangxi and they were forced to pull back. This led them on a long retreat—during which many people joined in, and they came to be identified by the people as the future leaders of China. So their destiny had nothing at all to do with the retreat from Jiangxi.

Or, to put it another way: From the perspective of history, the Chinese were not retreating at all.

They were just, well...walking forward behind themselves!

The energy of your experience is an open system.

☆   ☆   ☆

This brings up another aspect of faith: Faith in intelligent movement and commitment to the moment. If we can trust that we belong where we are at a given moment, we'll learn the lessons we need to learn there *faster* than if we resist.

One of the most respected scientific thinkers of all time was the philosopher Alfred North Whitehead. He pointed out that we see objects in Newtonian terms, as fixed in time and space, but they aren't.

> *The universe is not a museum with its*
> *specimens in glass cases. — Whitehead*

Fixed in time and space: I am at Point A, (college graduate). I am looking to move through time and space to Point B (the end-point; my future) and I want to know in advance what I'll find there.

It is nonsense to conceive of nature as a static fact...There is no nature apart from transition ...That is the reason why the notion of an instant of time, conceived as a primary simple fact, is nonsense. — Whitehead

Like the secret agent who's told to go to a pick-up spot in three weeks time and get the envelope with further instructions, we have to trust that if we're doing the best we can, as intelligently as we can, the information we need will come to us—but it will do so when we need it, rather than beforehand.

And cycling back to the first paragraph of the book, let's say you don't know what you want to do for your career, or you do know, but you don't know how to get there. Faith in movement means that it's realistic to think it over and then to begin. Period. To take a step, guided by your highest possible awareness at the time.

Trust that once you put your foot in the stream of motion, in the best way you can, according to your best perception at the time, the stream will take you places. You can further trust that the places it will take you are related to where you'll eventually want to be. And that when you need to make a turn or adjustment in your course, you'll know.

We experience more than we can analyze.
— Alfred North Whitehead

☆   ☆   ☆

Finally, there's the question of what step to take.

I know someone who has a hard time making decisions. She may accept in her head that movement is important, but she still finds it tough to choose between Option A and Option B. And once she chooses, she worries that she has made a mistake.

I used to be that way, but I once read about a scientific theory that helped me. The theory comes from the branch of physics known as quantum mechanics.

Before getting to the theory, I'd like to mention one small qualifying factor: The laws of quantum mechanics apply to things on the microcosmic level. In other words, this theory may be more meaningful if you were an amoeba or an electron rather than someone named Alex or Stephanie. But in my opinion, even if these laws are not proven to apply to macrocosmic entities like us, they ring true and can be helpful when taken symbolically, if not literally.

The theory is this: "Contrafactual Definiteness" doesn't exist.

What it implies: If you have two choices, and you think about what each one would involve, and then you decide to take one rather than the other, you can no longer assume that what you predicted for the other would still apply.

So let's say on a Saturday night you're deciding what to do. You can either go out to a movie or stay home and read a book. You think about it for a while, and finally decide to stay home. Then the next day you read that there was a fire in the movie theater and many people died. Your logical reaction may be, "Whew! What a tragedy! Thank God I stayed home. If I had gone to the movie, I might have been killed."

However, this theory states that all you can assume is one thing: You're glad you stayed home. And you'd have to stop your analysis right there.

The second part, that you might have been killed, is a fantasy. In other words, you can't assume that if you'd gone, there would have been a fire—because if you'd gone, you would have changed the alignment, much as a butterfly flapping its wings on one side of the world can eventually cause a hurricane on the other, according to the Butterfly Effect in Chaos Theory. Or better still, the "It's a Wonderful Life"-Jimmy Stewart effect.

Does this sound too wild?

Well, let's say that once upon a time, you were choosing between two schools, Universities A and B. University A accepted you and University B didn't. Then, during your first semester at A, you started thinking "If I'd gone to B, I know that I would have played soccer," or "I would have made the Dean's list," or whatever else you might have told yourself.

But here's the thing: Who knows what would have happened had you gone to University B? Anything. You might have broken your leg on B's slippery steps in the snow and you wouldn't have played soccer. Or you might have met someone, changed all your ideas about your life and future, and moved to Australia.

There it is. The theory of Contrafactual Definitiveness. Once you decide to go to University A, your ideas about University B and what would have happened there are unreliable. If you make a decision, know that the what-ifs are something of an empty fantasy.

It works for me.

☆　　☆　　☆

END NOTES

Sources of Longer Quotations:

–Peter F. Drucker, from *Management: Tasks Responsibilities Practices* (1993; Harperbusiness) (Perspective)
–Alfred North Whitehead, from *Modes of Thought* (1938; The Free Press) (Faith In Yourself)
–Marianne Williamson, from *A Return to Love* (1992; Harper Collins) (Relationships)
–Oprah Winfrey, from commencement address, Salem College, Winston-Salem, North Carolina (New York Times, May 29, 2000) (Career)

Bill Gates, Letter to computer hobbyists. February 1973. In "An Open Letter to Hobbyists," Computer Notes, February 3, 1976, p.4. Reprinted by permission of Microsoft.

Additional gratitude to Gary Zukav's quantum mechanics primer *The Dancing Wu Li Masters* for the judge joke and introducing me to contrafactual definitiveness, and to Morris Berman's moving *The Reenchantment of the World*, which included Bateson's illustration of the Double Bind Box.

Additional Reading:
–On the Inner Perspective and changing beliefs, some may find Anthony Robbin's *Awaken the Giant Within* helpful, as well as the field of Neuro-Linguistic Programming (NLP).
–On relationships, some may find Eva Pierrakos and Judith Saly's esoteric *Creating Union* helpful.

I'd like to thank Bette Jedding, Caroline Kepnes, Mark Levy, Terry Rosenberg, Donald Sanders, and Steve Wood for their encouragement and support.

To order, send check (or credit card #, name, exp date) for $15.95 plus $2.00 shipping (in N.Y. add 1.32/total 3.32) to Double Rose Books P.O. Box 180, New York, N.Y. 10276-0180 Include name, address, (shipping name and address if different, gift message), phone, e-mail if applicable.
Or phone orders to: 800 253-4992 Fax: 212 228-6632

Reallifenotes.com